INTERNATIONAL
MONETARY REFORM
AND
THE DEVELOPING
COUNTRIES

WILLIAM R. CLINE

INTERNATIONAL MONETARY REFORM AND THE DEVELOPING COUNTRIES

THE BROOKINGS INSTITUTION

Washington, D.C.

Library of Congress Cataloging in Publication Data:
Cline, William R
   International monetary reform and the developing
countries.
   Includes bibliographical references and index.
      1. Underdeveloped areas—Foreign exchange problem.
2. Special drawing rights.   3. Economic assistance.
I. Title.
HG3890.C54   332.4'5   75-44503
ISBN 0-8157-1476-9
ISBN 0-8157-1475-0 pbk.

1 2 3 4 5 6 7 8 9

THE BROOKINGS INSTITUTION is an independent organization devoted to nonpartisan research, education, and publication in economics, government, foreign policy, and the social sciences generally. Its principal purposes are to aid in the development of sound public policies and to promote public understanding of issues of national importance.

The Institution was founded on December 8, 1927, to merge the activities of the Institute for Government Research, founded in 1916, the Institute of Economics, founded in 1922, and the Robert Brookings Graduate School of Economics and Government, founded in 1924.

The Board of Trustees is responsible for the general administration of the Institution, while the immediate direction of the policies, program, and staff is vested in the President, assisted by an advisory committee of the officers and staff. The by-laws of the Institution state: "It is the function of the Trustees to make possible the conduct of scientific research, and publication, under the most favorable conditions, and to safeguard the independence of the research staff in the pursuit of their studies and in the publication of the results of such studies. It is not a part of their function to determine, control, or influence the conduct of particular investigations or the conclusions reached."

The President bears final responsibility for the decision to publish a manuscript as a Brookings book. In reaching his judgment on the competence, accuracy, and objectivity of each study, the President is advised by the director of the appropriate research program and weighs the views of a panel of expert outside readers who report to him in confidence on the quality of the work. Publication of a work signifies that it is deemed a competent treatment worthy of public consideration but does not imply endorsement of conclusions or recommendations.

The Institution maintains its position of neutrality on issues of public policy in order to safeguard the intellectual freedom of the staff. Hence interpretations or conclusions in Brookings publications should be understood to be solely those of the authors and should not be attributed to the Institution, to its trustees, officers, or other staff members, or to the organizations that support its research.

Foreword

IN AUGUST 1971 the United States suspended convertibility of the dollar into gold; in the following December the Group of Ten signed the Smithsonian Agreement realigning exchange rates and devaluing the dollar. By February 1973 a second devaluation of the dollar had become necessary, and soon thereafter the major currencies shifted to a regime of floating exchange rates. These events spelled the end of the Bretton Woods international monetary system, which had functioned well during most of the postwar period.

As the search for a new system began, the developing countries demanded and received representation in the formal bodies established for monetary reform negotiations—first the Committee of Twenty and later the Interim Committee of the International Monetary Fund. Negotiations culminated in the Jamaica agreements reached by the Interim Committee in January 1976. By then negotiators had agreed to revise IMF rules to permit floating exchange rates and to establish coordination procedures intended to moderate exchange rate fluctuations; to abolish the official price of gold and allow central banks to buy and sell gold at market prices; to sell some of the gold held by the IMF and to use the profits for development aid; and to redefine the Special Drawing Right. Now it seems likely that there will be a period of reflection and review as countries ratify agreements and gain experience in operating under the new conditions.

Nevertheless, the developing countries, buffeted by the dollar devaluations and floating exchange rates, remain preoccupied with two issues: the degree of exchange rate flexibility and how—or whether—aid should be linked to SDR creation. An analysis of these two issues forms the substance of this book. Addressing himself to a variety of interrelated questions, the author concludes that the developing countries are more likely to gain than lose from the movement of industrial countries to flexible exchange rates; that an SDR aid link, if focused on the poorest countries, could be a helpful but modest aid mechanism once the creation of more SDRs is again needed, although in the author's view world liquidity is now adequate or excessive; and that the developing countries have achieved important successes in the negotiations to date.

William R. Cline, a senior fellow in the Brookings Foreign Policy Studies program, wishes to thank the following individuals for their helpful comments: Stanley W. Black, C. Fred Bergsten, Ralph C. Bryant, Carlos Díaz-Alejandro, Charles R. Frank, Jr., Edward R. Fried, Irving S. Friedman, Gottfried Haberler, Arnold C. Harberger, Gerald K. Helleiner, Anthony Lanyi, Walter S. Salant, Robert Solomon, Thomas D. Willett, and John Williamson. Robert Williams provided research assistance for the study; Barbara P. Haskins edited the manuscript; it was checked for factual accuracy by Laurel Rabin and Eileen Dripchak, and typed by Marie Hanks. The index was prepared by Florence Robinson.

This project was financed by the U.S. Agency for International Development through a program of collaborative research between Brookings and the Secretariat of the Central American Common Market. The program provides for research on general problems of economic development as well as joint research on issues of economic integration in Central America.

The views presented in this book are those of the author and should not be ascribed to the persons or organizations whose assistance is acknowledged above, or to the trustees, officers, or other staff members of the Brookings Institution.

GILBERT Y. STEINER
Acting President

March 1976
Washington, D.C.

Contents

CHAPTER ONE

Introduction

THE INTERNATIONAL MONETARY SYSTEM is the set of government practices and market forces that determine rates of exchange among national currencies and holdings of reserves of internationally acceptable assets. For several decades before World War I this system, for the major western countries, was based on the gold standard. These countries maintained convertibility of their currencies into gold at fixed par values. A country with a balance of payments deficit tended to lose gold, which reduced domestic money supply and put downward pressure on domestic money income and prices—providing the basis for automatic correction in the payments balance as the country's goods became more attractive to foreign buyers and foreign goods less attractive to domestic residents.

In the face of inflation during World War I convertibility into gold broke down, but by the late nineteen twenties major countries had reestablished convertibility and fixed exchange rates. Countries now began to hold more and more reserves in pounds sterling in addition to gold, so that the gold standard became a gold exchange standard. However, the fixed rates of the late nineteen twenties proved to be seriously overvalued for the pound and undervalued for other currencies, particularly the French franc. In 1931 the gold exchange standard collapsed when Britain, under pressure to redeem large foreign balances of sterling for gold, suspended convertibility into gold. The world depression of the nineteen thirties complicated return to a stable monetary system, as countries refused to accept further price deflation to achieve balance of payments correction, engaged in competitive devaluation in attempts to stimulate employment through export expansion, and raised tariff barriers against imports. Frequent and fruitless changes in exchange rates in this period led many ob-

1

servers to conclude that flexible rates were incompatible with a stable monetary system.[1]

The Bretton Woods agreements in 1944 resurrected the gold exchange standard, this time with the dollar and sterling as key currencies supplementing gold as internationally acceptable assets. Mindful of the competitive devaluations, which marked the nineteen thirties, participants in the Bretton Woods conference sought a return to a system with fixed par values that could be changed only under conditions of fundamental disequilibrium. To facilitate the maintenance of these exchange rates the agreements provided for the creation of the International Monetary Fund, which would make loans to countries in short-term balance of payments difficulties. For nearly three decades the gold exchange system functioned successfully; international trade grew rapidly, tariff barriers were reduced by a series of trade negotiations, and by the end of the nineteen fifties the major currencies were made freely convertible into foreign exchange.

Collapse of the Bretton Woods System

By the early nineteen sixties economists were already warning that the accumulation of key currency reserves was undermining the stability of the world monetary system. This accumulation required steady balance of payments deficits of the key currency countries, of which the United States was the most important. As the foreign exchange reserves grew the liquid liabilities of the key currency countries became large relative to their gold stocks available for conversion, threatening a weakening of the key currencies.[2] Furthermore, the absence of flexibility in exchange rates under the system meant that distortions gathered force over long periods of time rather than being relieved from time to time by changes in exchange rates. Fixed rates also gave speculators an easy target since there was only one direction in which a rate under pressure would be likely to move if authorities were unable to maintain it.

Pressure on the dollar intensified during the late nineteen sixties as the United States experienced increasing rates of inflation. Arrangements pro-

1. For example, see Ragnar Nurkse, *International Currency Experience* (League of Nations, 1944). For a concise historical review of the international monetary system, see Robert Triffin, *The Evolution of the International Monetary System: Historical Reappraisal and Future Perspectives,* Studies in International Finance 12 (Princeton University, International Finance Section, 1964).

2. Robert Triffin, *Gold and the Dollar Crisis* (Yale University Press, 1960).

liferated providing for emergency swaps of currencies and for voluntary restraint by foreign central banks in the conversion of their dollar holdings into gold. Aside from these ad hoc measures the only revision in the monetary system in this period was the agreement in 1967 to establish Special Drawing Rights (SDRs) as a new source of international liquidity free from the resource costs of gold mined from the ground and from the special problems of liquidity creation through foreign exchange reserves. Even this instrument was created in a context in which one important motive appeared to be to provide a breathing space for the dollar and pound by supplying extra liquidity to the United States and the United Kingdom.

The Bretton Woods system ended on August 15, 1971, when in response to intolerable balance of payments deterioration the United States suspended convertibility of the dollar into gold and imposed a 10 percent surcharge on imports.[3] In the months that followed the United States encouraged other countries to appreciate their currencies, while the other countries insisted upon a devaluation of the dollar in relation to gold. The Smithsonian realignment of exchange rates in December 1971 represented a compromise, whereby the dollar devalued vis-à-vis gold; the franc, pound, and other currencies remained at their original parity with gold; and the strongest currencies—the deutsche mark, yen, and Swiss franc—appreciated with respect to gold.

Monetary Reform Efforts

The obvious need to improve the faltering international monetary system and the demand that the poor countries be represented in international monetary negotiations led in mid-1972 to the establishment of the Committee on Reform of the International Monetary System of the IMF Board of Governors—the "Committee of Twenty." Representation in this body was broadly along the lines of that in the International Monetary Fund. In addition to the major industrial countries, the committee included nine developing countries, each of which in turn represented a cluster of other developing countries.[4]

3. Some would argue that this decision was taken with the objective of reducing domestic unemployment through the expansion of exports. (C. Fred Bergsten, "The New Economics and U.S. Foreign Policy," *Foreign Affairs*, January 1972, pp. 199–222.)

4. The Committee of Twenty included delegates from Argentina, Australia, Bel-

For two years the Committee of Twenty assessed the structural reforms required for the international monetary system. The principal issues were: (a) the appropriate degree of flexibility in exchange rates for accomplishing balance of payments adjustment; (b) the need for greater symmetry in the system, between pressures for adjustment on surplus and on deficit countries, on the one hand, and between reserve centers and nonreserve currencies, on the other; (c) the return to convertibility into reserve assets for the dollar and pound sterling, and a decision on whether convertibility should be automatic or voluntary; and (d) the nature of future international reserve assets.

The deliberations generated consensus on some issues. Greater exchange rate flexibility than under the Bretton Woods system was agreed to be essential; the exchange rate regime would be based on "stable but adjustable par values and with floating rates recognized as providing a useful technique in particular situations."[5] The SDR would become the principal reserve asset and the role of gold and reserve currencies would be reduced. Valuation of the SDR was changed from a specified amount of gold to a specified basket of currencies, and the interest rate on the SDR was raised. Agreement also was reached on guidelines for floating. Considerable variance of viewpoint remained, however, on several issues, including the criteria for judging when balance of payments adjustment was needed and especially the role that should be assigned to reserves and reserve changes as indicators of the need for adjustment action; the form of convertibility; the future role of gold, especially whether or not monetary authorities should be authorized to buy and sell to each other, or even buy from the market, at a market-related price; whether and on what terms and conditions a facility should be established in the Fund for the "consolidation" of outstanding reserve currency balances in exchange for SDRs; and whether a linkage should be established between development assistance and the creation of SDRs (the "SDR aid link").

During the deliberations of the Committee of Twenty three major developments occurred in the international economy that profoundly influenced the atmosphere in which the negotiations took place. First, after

gium, Brazil, Canada, Ethiopia, France, Germany, India, Indonesia, Iraq, Italy, Japan, Morocco, the Netherlands, Sweden, the United States, the United Kingdom, Venezuela, and Zaire. Most of these delegates represented several countries in addition to their own.

5. International Monetary Fund, Committee on Reform of the International Monetary System and Related Issues (Committee of Twenty), *International Monetary Reform: Documents of the Committee of Twenty* (IMF, 1974), p. 8.

massive dollar outflows in early 1973 the United States devalued a second time in relation to gold (resulting in a devaluation by 10 percent with respect to the major currencies). Shortly thereafter, as outflows of capital continued, the United States and the other major industrial countries moved to a regime of floating exchange rates with intervention by monetary authorities. Second, the increase in oil prices in late 1973 and early 1974 brought an enormous shift in world trade and payment flows. Third, in 1973 and 1974 world inflation accelerated to rates far above those previously experienced throughout the postwar period. Because of the uncertainty associated with these developments, and because of the persistence of differing opinions on fundamental issues, the committee reached no final agreements on monetary reform.

Subsequent negotiations on international monetary reform took place in the International Monetary Fund's Interim Committee of the Board of Governors on the International Monetary System. In August of 1975 this Committee reached an important agreement designed to reduce the role of gold in the international monetary system while aiding the developing countries. The agreement provided that the official price of gold would be abolished; that one-sixth of the IMF's gold holdings would be sold, with the profit going to the developing countries; and that another sixth would be returned to members. In November of 1975 the heads of state from France, Germany, Italy, Japan, the United Kingdom, and the United States met at Rambouillet, France, and resolved the impasse (primarily between the United States and France) on floating exchange rates. The Interim Committee's meeting in Jamaica in January 1976 marked the end of the negotiations for at least the first stage of monetary reform. The Jamaica agreements provided for amendments to the IMF's Articles of Agreement legitimizing floating exchange rates and incorporating the other elements of reform previously agreed upon (including those concerning gold and changes in IMF quotas). These amendments now must be ratified by national legislatures, a process that could require up to two years to complete.

Interests of the Developing Countries

To the developing countries the turbulence in the international monetary system beginning in 1971 meant new complications and possible losses in a situation already made difficult by stagnation in the real flows of development assistance. The optimism of the "development decade" of the nineteen sixties, a period of activist aid programs such as the Alliance for Progress of the United States, had already given way to a growing atmosphere of pessimism and confrontation with the rich countries in forums such as the United Nations Conference on Trade and Development (UNCTAD). Emerging demands of the developing countries for measures, such as an aid target of 1 percent of the gross national products of the industrial countries and tariff preferences for developing countries, remained unresolved issues.

Suspension of gold convertibility by the United States in 1971 represented a unilateral action with repercussions on the developing countries, especially those with a large portion of their reserves held in dollars. Similarly, the developing countries had little role in the negotiations among the major industrial countries leading to the Smithsonian realignment of exchange rates in December of 1971. In reaction to this exclusion the LDCs began organizing into groups to present a united front in demanding representation in international monetary decisions. They pressed these demands in forums such as the third meeting of UNCTAD in Santiago, Chile, in 1972. The demand for active participation in decisionmaking was finally met by the inclusion of LDC representatives in the formal body established in the IMF for the monetary reform negotiations, the Committee of Twenty.

In substantive terms the developing countries organized a united demand that monetary reform include a new mechanism linking the creation of SDRs to development assistance. The concept of giving the LDCs a larger portion of internationally created liquidity than they would receive from allocation of SDRs proportional to their IMF quotas had existed for several years and had been an issue at the time of the original agreement establishing the SDR. It was natural that, with the international monetary system now completely open for revision, and under the perception that outside monetary forces had dealt them economic losses, the LDCs pressed the demand for an aid link as part of a reformed system. The faltering of aid flows under more conventional forms only enhanced the appeal of supplementing the development assistance effort with a mechanism of the international monetary system.

Of all the other issues involved in the reform negotiations, the single element of greatest concern to the LDCs was the degree of flexibility in exchange rates among industrial countries. Although their positions were less uniform on this issue, the developing countries tended to oppose much greater flexibility of exchange rates among the industrial countries, essentially because they believed that increased fluctuation of these rates would introduce a whole new dimension of uncertainty into an already very uncertain international economic milieu that made the preparation and execution of their own development plans extremely difficult.

The monetary reform agreements reached at Jamaica and before did not include a linkage between SDRs and development assistance. While negotiators from the LDCs criticized this omission,[6] they nevertheless went along with the agreements on other issues. The proposal on sales of gold held by the IMF meant direct benefits for the developing countries (although some of their representatives feared that the final result of the revisions affecting gold would be to raise the effective price of gold reserves, thus conferring a windfall gain primarily on the industrial countries that own the bulk of official gold holdings). LDC representatives were probably willing to accept the other major change in the monetary system —incorporation of floating exchange rates into accepted practice under IMF rules—because it represented little more than de jure recognition of a de facto reality. Furthermore, the agreement provided for new procedures of intercountry consultations to facilitate the smoothing out of erratic fluctuations in exchange rates.

The purpose of this study is to explore in depth the implications of international monetary reform for the developing countries. Chapter 2 discusses the advantages and disadvantages for LDCs of a system with substantially more flexible exchange rates among industrial countries than under the Bretton Woods system. (The findings therefore bear directly on the monetary system that has now evolved.) Chapter 3 examines the arguments for and against linking SDR emissions to development assistance, and therefore concerns an outstanding issue that may or may not be resolved in future monetary reform negotiations. The chapter also discusses the provision of aid to developing countries through sales of gold held by the IMF. Finally, chapter 4 investigates the adequacy of world reserves, in view of the crucial relevance of this question for determining whether any SDRs should be created at all, and therefore whether an SDR aid link would be helpful to LDCs.

6. International Monetary Fund, *IMF Survey,* January 19, 1976, p. 29.

CHAPTER TWO

Flexible Exchange Rates and the Developing Countries

A CRUCIAL ELEMENT in international monetary reform is improvement in the balance of payments adjustment process. There is widespread agreement that this improvement requires more flexible exchange rates than under the Bretton Woods system, and the Jamaica agreement legitimizes flexible rates. Yet there have been objections that greater exchange rate flexibility will be detrimental to the less developed countries, as well as claims that the LDCs have already been injured by the Smithsonian realignment of exchange rates in December 1971, the February 1973 dollar devaluation, and the floating of major currencies thereafter.

This chapter first examines the attitudes of LDCs toward exchange rate flexibility and the logical arguments concerning the differential impact of flexibility on LDCs. It then reviews the empirical evidence on effects experienced by LDCs to date and on the actual exchange rate practices followed by developing countries in the face of currency realignments and floating rates among the industrial countries. The objective of this examination is to determine how the interests of the LDCs are likely to be affected by flexibility, and whether they should be accorded special treatment in a reformed monetary system to offset any identified disadvantages attributable to flexibility.

Actual experience with floating rates since 1973 does not provide an ideal test of the impact on LDCs of a planned floating rate system. Floating exchange rates have existed by default rather than design. Monetary authorities have generally agreed that recent disturbances caused by the oil price rise, rampant inflation, and volatile flows of short-term capital ruled out the fixing of exchange rates. Parities set under these unstable conditions would very probably prove to be unsustainable. Yet a return to a par value system remains a goal for many countries. Even as the Jamaica agreement legalized floating rates (under the oblique phrase, "other exchange arrangements of a member's choice"), it kept the door open for "the introduction of a widespread system of exchange arrangements based on stable but adjustable par values" upon determination by an 85 percent majority of IMF voting power.[1]

A dominant official viewpoint (although not one shared by the United States) is that the experience of 1973 and after showed that allowing exchange rates to float in response to market forces is unsatisfactory. According to this viewpoint, because trade values initially respond slowly or even perversely to exchange rate moves, floating could bring greater exchange rate swings than justified for equilibrium over the medium and longer terms.[2] However, the official goal of fixed rates with more frequent parity changes has been challenged on grounds that it would lead once again to massive reserve movements as governments attempted to hold their currencies, even temporarily, to agreed exchange rate relationships with each other.[3] Of course, flexible rates do not at present float freely but are "managed," with governments intervening when they wish to influence rates operating under the loose intervention guidelines of the International Monetary Fund, and this will continue to be the case under the agreements negotiated in Jamaica.

Flexible Rates for Developing Countries Themselves: Pros and Cons

The central issue of this chapter is the indirect effect of flexible exchange rates among industrial countries on the LDCs. However, it is important to consider briefly the issue of flexibility in the exchange rates of

1. Proposed amendment of Article IV of the IMF Articles of Agreement as reported in International Monetary Fund, *IMF Survey*, January 19, 1976, p. 20.

2. H. Johannes Witteveen, "Presentation of the Twenty-eighth Annual Report," in International Monetary Fund, *Summary Proceedings of the Twenty-eighth Annual Meeting of the Board of Governors* (IMF, 1973), pp. 20–21. (These annual summaries are hereinafter referred to as IMF, *Summary Proceedings*.) Even those officials who dislike floating would probably generally agree that it has been the only realistic option given the very unsettled conditions of the period since early 1973.

3. Gottfried Haberler, *Two Essays on the Future of the International Monetary Order*, American Enterprise Institute for Public Policy Research, Reprint 21 (Washington, D.C.: AEI, 1974).

the LDCs themselves. Several developing countries appear to prefer fixed rates among industrial countries but flexibility for their own rates. From their viewpoint, this combination would lessen the uncertainty associated with flexible rates among industrial countries and at the same time preserve their own freedom to stimulate exports and offset domestic inflationary policy, as illustrated most notably by the Brazilian "trotting peg."[4]

There is much to be said for allowing flexibility of LDC exchange rates even if it is given that industrial country rates are to be fixed. The chronic malady of the LDCs' foreign economic activity has in many cases been the maintenance of unrealistic exchange rates in the face of high domestic inflation. In these circumstances the risk imposed on the exporter by infrequent but very large exchange rate devaluations—made finally inevitable by inflation—has contributed to the stagnation of export supply and hence to the "trade gap" that has hindered growth. Moreover, as more developing countries demonstrate success in aggressive export expansion policies employing devaluation and other measures, the longstanding myth that devaluation will not benefit LDC balance of payments because demand for their exports is inelastic has become obsolete. Recent empirical studies by Cooper and by Connolly and Taylor provide evidence that devaluation does improve the developing country's balance of payments.[5]

There is of course an entire set of developing countries for whom devaluation is anathema. They vehemently support unchanged parities in relation to their respective traditional industrial country trading partners in the belief that devaluation will do nothing to help their balance of payments, but that devaluation will provoke inflation and worsen the terms of trade. In addition, there are often political considerations that rule out devaluation; authorities in some LDCs fear that devaluation would demonstrate loss of government control, and would shake confidence of

4. In the late 1960s Brazil initiated a policy of mini-devaluations at very frequent periods in order to maintain relatively constant real incentives for exports in the face of persistent high rates of domestic inflation. This regime has been called the trotting peg because of the frequency and size of peg adjustments.

5. Richard N. Cooper, *Currency Devaluations in Developing Countries,* Essays in International Finance 86 (Princeton University, International Finance Section, 1971); Michael B. Connolly and Dean J. Taylor, "Devaluation in Less Developed Countries," Paper prepared for the December 1971 conference on devaluation sponsored by the Board of Governors, Federal Reserve System (Washington, D.C., 1972; processed).

foreign investors and precipitate capital flight. Countries such as Mexico, some Central American countries, India, and many African countries apparently subscribe to this view.

Several major developing countries have turned to flexible or quasi-flexible rates, including Brazil, Colombia, Indonesia, Korea, Malaysia, Morocco, the Philippines, Yugoslavia, and Vietnam (see pages 42 and 43, table 2-4). It is undoubtedly true that rates in most of these countries do not float freely. They are managed by the monetary authorities and changed gradually (under "crawling peg" or "trotting peg" adjustment). It is unclear whether free floating would be an advantage for them. LDC economies are generally subject to more nonmarket control and government interventions than industrial countries; they tend to have greater export price fluctuations, and more severe shocks to their foreign sectors as individual policies (such as expropriation and profits remittance control) are changed. The temporary swings associated with pure floating would thus seem to constitute a greater danger for LDC exchange regimes than for those of developed countries. The main utility of flexibility for these LDCs, then, is more likely to be that the crawling peg system can maintain constant real export and import incentives in the face of domestic rates of inflation different from the average for the rest of the world.

In relation to the major issues discussed below, an important problem confronting LDCs as a result of more flexible exchange rates among the major world currencies is how to respond to this flexibility in the setting of their own exchange rates. The existence of a growing bloc of LDCs gaining expertise in dealing with their own exchange rate flexibility suggests that at least these countries should be well prepared to deal with the policy choices posed by flexibility among advanced countries in a reformed international system. Moreover, in view of the generally favorable effect on the foreign sector of greater flexibility in their own rates in these countries, it would represent a step backward if monetary reform measures seeking a return to a par value system forced LDCs to return to more rigid exchange rates than is now the case. However, the precedent of exemption, or nonreciprocity, for LDCs in other contexts, such as in past and current trade negotiations within the General Agreement on Tariffs and Trade and the generalized system of tariff preferences, could be invoked to permit exemptions from such rules for the LDCs.

Flexible Rates among Developed Countries: LDC Attitudes

The developing countries have generally opposed greater exchange rate flexibility. Historically, they appear to have identified "flexibility" with the probable devaluation of the pound if it were permitted to float. As a consequence, many Commonwealth countries anticipated that such an occurrence would reduce the real value of their export earnings from commodities whose prices were quoted in sterling.[6] During the monetary crises and eventual realignment of 1971, the LDC reaction was more generally one of frustration at exogenous shocks imposed on them by shifts in major currency parities. LDC representatives at international meetings, including the third meeting of the United Nations Conference on Trade and Development (UNCTAD III), emphasized their countries' loss of real value of dollar reserves, as well as of sterling reserves (which had in vain been given a dollar parity guarantee), and the rise in dollar costs of imports from Japan and Europe. The same spokesmen were undoubtedly aware of, but made little reference to, the decline in real value of their outstanding debt denominated in dollars (although they did point out the rise in real cost of their nondollar debt). Moreover, they foresaw no compensating increase in dollar prices of their commodity exports.

When discussions on monetary reform began in the Committee of Twenty, LDC participants tended to support fixity of exchange rates rather than substantially greater flexibility.[7] This position was no doubt influenced by their perceptions of possible injury from the Smithsonian realignment as well as their concern that greater flexibility meant greater uncertainty generally and made their own monetary and development planning decisions more difficult. Yet the general floating of exchange

6. I am indebted to Irving S. Friedman for this observation. Note that the concern probably also applied to Latin American countries, in view of dollar quotations for the area's primary products and the likelihood of a devaluation of the dollar if rates were to float, beginning in the 1960s.

7. The IMF 1972 report on monetary reform states: "with respect to international monetary arrangements in general, the LDCs have for the most part expressed a strong preference for the par value system, with narrow rather than wider margins"; in International Monetary Fund, *Reform of the International Monetary System,* a Report by the Executive Directors to the Board of Governors (IMF, 1972), p. 69.

rates and the rapid inflation of 1973 appear to have made the modest increments in flexibility considered in the formal reform proposals look quite tame by comparison. By the time of the 1973 IMF and World Bank annual meetings, LDC opposition to increased flexibility in a revised system appeared to have weakened. Their goal by then was a termination of floating but not a return to the rigidity of fixed rates under the Bretton Woods system.[8]

Thus, although the 1973 meetings reflected a general concern that LDCs in particular had been injured by the currency floats (with the most dramatic declarations being made, ironically, by non-LDC spokesmen[9]), a representative of the monetarily conservative West African Monetary Union could say:

... we consider that the new monetary order should:
—lead to a system of parities that are fixed but adjustable within reasonable limits which, while abandoning the extreme rigidity of former years, would avoid the laxity of the present by stabilizing the exchange market. The present system of floating which seemed to hold promise for a moment is now clearly outdated; in the future, floating should only be an exceptional recourse authorized by the Fund alone.[10]

Despite the persistent ongoing fears of the LDCs that a world system of flexible, and especially floating, rates would have negative effects on their economies,[11] in the end their negotiators went along with the incorporation of flexible rates into accepted practice under IMF rules. It is important to examine the bases of the arguments that greater exchange rate flexibility in the world monetary system may be detrimental to the LDCs.

8. These observations draw upon discussions with developing country experts familiar with the evolution of the committee's deliberations.

9. IMF Managing Director H. Johannes Witteveen and Anthony Barber for the United Kingdom in IMF, *Summary Proceedings* (1973), pp. 21, 42. One suspects that pleading the case for the LDCs provided a convenient cover for some officials' own preferences on the issue of flexibility.

10. Edouard Kodjo in ibid., p. 185.

11. For example, the statement by Guinea at the 1973 IMF and World Bank meetings expresses one such fear: "It is envisaged that future exchange rates will be 'stable but adjustable.' In other words, the margins of fluctuations of currencies will be much more elastic than in the past. It is to be feared that this is nothing more than the institutionalization of a concerted currency float. In that case it would not be favorable to the young nations, which will have scarcely any stable prices either for the goods they export or for those they import." (N'Faly Sangaré in ibid., pp. 90–91.)

Theoretical Considerations

The theoretical arguments put forward by those opposed to greater exchange rate flexibility among industrial nations because it might be detrimental to the interests of the LDCs are: (1) it would increase uncertainty about real export earnings, import prices, and foreign exchange reserve values; (2) it would lead to greater commodity price fluctuations; (3) it would encourage the formation of currency blocs and might inhibit the diversification of LDC trade from traditional trading partners; (4) it would raise problems for reserve and debt management; and (5) it would require the development of forward exchange markets, which would be difficult to establish in LDCs.

After examination of these issues below, it is concluded that these fears generally warrant little weight compared with the overriding factor of potential improvement in LDC exports and economic activity to be expected from the improvement in the world trade and financial system that could follow from more flexible exchange rates. In the case of some of the arguments, analysis is presented suggesting that their theoretical basis is weak. In the case of others, practical remedies are suggested for minimizing the seriousness of the problems cited.

The Uncertainty Issue

A central theme of the opposition of LDCs to greater exchange rate flexibility among developed countries is that the change would increase uncertainty. However, the general issue of increased uncertainty about export and import prices cannot meaningfully be analyzed by comparing a system of flexible exchange rates against one of eternally fixed, unchanging exchange rates. The latter is not a realistic option. In an ideal world with perfect upward and downward price and wage flexibility and smoothly functioning compensatory financing among countries, perpetually fixed exchange rates would be possible, and they would provide the welfare benefit of complete certainty about the foreign exchange rate. But in the real world these conditions are not met; indeed, an attempt to hold exchange rates perpetually fixed would most probably require domestically unacceptable recessionary measures in deficit industrial countries, which if adopted would injure exports from developing countries. The choice is therefore not between permanently fixed exchange rates and flexible rates, but between fixed rates with infrequent but large disruptive exchange rate realignments and a system with more frequent but smaller rate changes. If it could be guaranteed that over a span of time the frequent smaller changes would constitute greater fundamental stability than that associated with the alternative of periodic large jumps of fixed rates, there would be a strong case favoring flexible rates over fixed rates to obtain the objective of reduced uncertainty. This point may be seen in terms of utility analysis under risk aversion.

RISK AVERSION ANALYSIS. Figure 2-1 presents the utility associated with wealth level for a risk-averse country.[12] Risk aversion should characterize the LDCs because of their low level of income. The country begins with wealth Oc and utility OC. Since it is averse to risk, the incremental utility associated with an increase in wealth is less than the decrease in utility associated with a decline in wealth of the same size (giving the curvature shown in the utility function). Small changes are strictly preferred over large changes. For example, a change of magnitude $\pm X$ (with equal probability of rise or fall) generates a decline in expected utility equal to $AC - CE$, whereas a smaller change, $\pm Y$, generates a smaller expected loss, $BC - CD$. Furthermore, the disutility of expected loss grows more than proportionately with the size of the change:

$$[(AC - CE)/(BC - CD)] > [X/Y].$$

Thus the issue of uncertainty is whether flexible rates actually do provide smaller rate changes than fixed rates and, if so, whether the greater frequency of changes under flexible rates negates the benefits derived from smaller changes. To answer the latter question it is necessary to introduce weights in proportion to the time span involved—fluctuation of the exchange rate between breakfast and lunch is of little interest, whereas a protracted rate shift from January to June is important. A persistent change in the rate affects real resource allocation decisions, whereas gyrations over a very short period mainly affect windfall transfers among participants in exchange market speculation.

Consider the alternatives pictured in figure 2-2. With fixed rates the exchange rate follows path A. Under flexible rates it follows path B. For both, the average rate over the planning horizon T_1 is $\overline{R}$.

---

12. Several of the realignment effects are wealth effects (for example, changes in the real value of debt and reserves).

Figure 2-1. *Welfare Effects of Changes in Wealth under Risk Aversion*

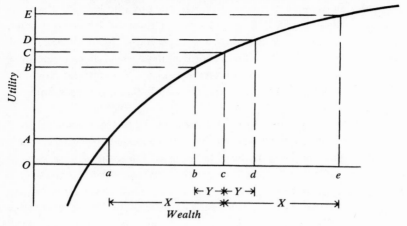

Figure 2-2. *Illustrative Movements of the Exchange Rate under Fixed- and Flexible-Rate Regimes*

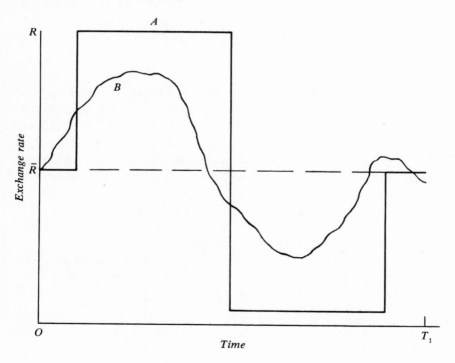

Table 2-1. *Mean, Standard Deviation, and Coefficient of Variation of Selected Currencies in Relation to the Dollar, 1959–75*[a]

Period and statistic	Germany (deutsche mark/ dollar)	Japan (yen/dollar)	Britain (dollar/ pound)	France (franc/ dollar)
Period of fixed rates, 1959:1–1973:1				
Mean	3.870	353.38	2.654	5.019
Standard deviation	0.305	19.94	0.188	0.235
Coefficient of variation	0.0789	0.0564	0.0707	0.0468
Period of floating rates, 1973:2–1975:1				
Mean	2.497	282.15	2.401	4.500
Standard deviation	0.130	12.47	0.077	0.275
Coefficient of variation	0.0519	0.0442	0.0321	0.0612

Source: Calculated from International Monetary Fund, *International Financial Statistics,* selected issues, end-of-quarter spot rates.

a. Based on quarterly data.

Now consider a cost function for fluctuation of the form:

(1)
$$ C = \int_{t=0}^{t=T_1} (R_t - \overline{R})^2 \, dt. $$

This function applies the time-span weighting desired, in the factor of integration *dt*. (In actual measurement, summation over discrete intervals replaces continuous integration.) The equation also incorporates increasing disutility of larger rate changes under risk aversion, by specifying the square of the deviation of exchange rate from period average (rather than merely the absolute deviation) as the penalty function.

If the choice between fixed and flexible rates is as shown, then the flexible rate provides lower uncertainty cost, because its deviations are not as extreme as those under fixed rates, and the minor short-period oscillations accompanying its underlying path (shown by the ripples in curve *B*) do not account for enough disturbance (after appropriate time-span weighting) to offset this advantage.

EMPIRICAL EVIDENCE ON RISK AVERSION. A crucial issue is whether the magnitudes of variation in exchange rates under flexibility will in fact be smaller than those associated with extended periods of fixed rates ending in major realignments. The empirical evidence on exchange rate variability under fixed and floating rates is shown in table 2-1 for the period between 1959 and 1975.

Since February 1973 the major currencies have been in a regime of managed floating. This period may therefore be considered as the reference period for data on the variability of floating rates. Fixed rates on the other hand extend back to the Bretton Woods agreements. However, a reasonable beginning date for examination of fixed rates is 1959. Prior to that year there were widespread practices of exchange controls even for European currencies, so that the performance of fixed rates is most accurately shown in the period following 1958. For the terminal point of the period of fixed rates the first quarter of 1973 is the reasonable demarcation. Hence, two major jolts—the Smithsonian realignment of rates in December 1971 and the February 1973 dollar devaluation—are appropriately included within this fixed-rate period.[13] Indeed, the purpose of testing the degree of exchange rate variability under fixed versus flexible exchange rate regimes would be lost if the wrenching adjustments at the end of a long period under fixed rates were excluded from the measurements for the period of fixed rates, since inflexibility is in large part responsible for the jolts.

The data on the mean, standard deviation, and coefficient of variation (ratio of standard deviation to mean) for the dollar quotation of the deutsche mark, yen, pound, and franc during the fixed and floating exchange rate periods are given in table 2-1. They indicate that, contrary to the popular impression, there were smaller underlying fluctuations during the period of floating rates than during the extended fixed-rate period. Except for the franc, the coefficient of variation[14] is higher for the fixed-rate period than for the floating-rate period. The data are for spot rates at the end of each quarter. This length of period for each observation is reasonable for assessing the variability of rates as viewed by producers and purchasers making decisions on production, imports, and exports. Similar results are obtained when monthly observations are used.[15] In contrast, daily quotations would hardly be relevant for the test. Day-by-day (or hour-to-hour) fluctuations are of little significance (just as day-to-day

13. Short interim periods of floating exchange rates for some individual currencies before the second quarter of 1973 are also included under the period of fixed rates.

14. Since the coefficient of variation derives from the variance, which increases as the square of the deviations from the mean, it is a relevant measure in terms of the features of increasing "penalty" for larger changes, that is, as shown in figure 2-1 and equation 1 above.

15. Based on calculations comparing 1971:1–1973:1 to 1973:2–1974:3.

movements cause little consternation for the longer-term private investor in the stock market).

Since experience with floating is quite limited to date, it would be inappropriate to interpret these results as conclusive evidence that floating generates greater fundamental certainty (that is, less fluctuation) than fixed rates.[16] A longer period of floating will be required before a more definitive comparison will be possible. However, it is striking that the evidence to date does contradict the general perception that floating rates have been more volatile than fixed rates. Moreover, the comparison is probably unfair to floating rates, for the following reasons. First, the experience begins from a base characterized by disequilibrium in the foreign exchange markets. Second, in this initial "learning" phase of early experience with floating, volatility was likely to be higher than might be expected eventually after exchange traders have become more familiar with floating and the exchange markets become more fully developed. Third, the heavy strains placed on the exchange markets by the changes in monetary flows associated with the oil price rise constitute another handicap imposed on the monetary system during the period for which the observations on floating rates are available.

As risk averters the LDCs should prefer frequent small changes in the exchange rates of developed countries over infrequent but very large changes. Preliminary evidence suggests that the variation in rates under floating has indeed been smaller than the shocks experienced under fixed rates, and this performance is all the more impressive considering the

---

16. In a study of the fluctuation of exchange rates from April 1973 through April 1974, Hirsch and Higham emphasize that volatility might have been reduced by better management of the flexible rates. However, they acknowledge that it is unclear whether the underlying fluctuation in rates has been greater under floating than under the fixed-rate regime, "particularly if the adjustments of summer 1971 and February–March 1973 are counted as a leftover of the adjustable peg period, which seems the reasonable interpretation." (Fred Hirsch and David Higham, "Floating Rates—Expectations and Experience," *The Three Banks Review*, no. 102 [June 1974], p. 17.)

A later study by Richard Blackhurst finds that the variability of exchange rates decreased very substantially in the year ending in June 1975 compared with the period January 1973 through June 1974. He attributes the improvement to an increase in central bank management of rates, the accumulation of experience by traders in the foreign exchange market, and the eventual approximation of rates toward equilibrium values from an initial disequilibrium base. (Richard Blackhurst, "Spot Market Variability under Floating Rates," *The Banker*, vol. 126 [January 1976], pp. 29–31.)

severe strains on exchange markets in the 1973–74 period due to the oil price increases. Nevertheless, it is too early to reach a reliable conclusion on the relative volatility of floating versus fixed rates.

OTHER ASPECTS OF UNCERTAINTY. Another important aspect of uncertainty concerns speculative capital flows, a dimension of "disruption" that is not apparent if exchange rates alone are examined. Large, infrequent changes in par values encourage disruptive speculation, because of the "one-way bet." Sufficiently small and frequent changes minimize these disruptive flows.[17] Indeed, in assessing the attempts of monetary reform to date, J. Marcus Fleming has called disruptive capital flows the Achilles' heel of reform; he seriously doubts that "anything short of heroic measures of recycling could make the par-value system viable in the presence of such flows, or that anything short of floating rates could check or canalize the flows and thus protect countries' monetary systems from external shocks."[18] To be sure, any injury suffered by LDCs from these flows is only indirect since the speculation involves "hot money" moving among industrial countries but not into LDCs. Nevertheless, the complex of capital controls and distortions in monetary policy resulting from attempts by industrial countries to control these movements is bound to inhibit the smooth expansion of markets for exports from the LDCs.

Another approach[19] to the uncertainty issue concerns the relationship of inflation to exchange rates among industrial countries. Without asserting a strict purchasing power parity theory, it should be reasonable to expect changes in exchange rates among these countries to be within the same orders of magnitude as their differences in inflation rates. Therefore, any uncertainty accompanying more flexible rates should merely replace uncertainty previously associated with differential inflation rates, causing no increase on balance in the uncertainty facing LDC planners. Moreover, if the flexibility behaves in strict adherence to constant "purchasing power parity," the underlying uncertainty is even reduced by the move to flexibility, since the real cost of imports from a given country is held constant as movements in the exchange rate exactly offset price movements.[20]

17. I am indebted to Gottfried Haberler for this alternative focus.

18. J. Marcus Fleming, *Reflections on the International Monetary Reform*, Essays in International Finance 107 (Princeton University, International Finance Section, 1974), pp. 13–14.

19. For which I am indebted to Arnold C. Harberger.

20. Suppose suppliers *A* and *B* both have initial exchange rates of one currency unit for each Special Drawing Right. Each supplies half of the LDC's imports, which are inelastic in the short run and therefore fixed in quantity regardless of price. Sup-

If differential inflation is ruled out but nevertheless forces exist causing swings in the balance of payments among industrial countries, there is reason why flexibility in rates among industrial countries may provoke disturbance in LDCs that would not occur under fixed rates. With fixed rates, temporary payments swings are accommodated by the shift of reserves from one developed country to another.[21] This "reserve quantity" adjustment does not affect LDCs (under optimistic assumptions that auxiliary measures such as import controls are not undertaken in the country losing reserves). In contrast, under flexible rates it is the trade "price"—the exchange rate—that moves rather than reserves. But this exchange rate is a price that affects all international transactions and values, and whose influence is therefore not isolated to the industrial countries directly involved.

THE CRUCIAL QUESTION is therefore whether crisis resolution by reserve shifts with fixed rates is a viable solution or whether it merely delays what will later be a large disruptive shift in exchange rates. In the latter case (considered above as the more realistic alternative), the crisis eventually inflicts itself on the LDCs despite the fixed-rate system, and does so in a more extreme realignment.

Commodity Price Fluctuation

A more specific fear of the LDCs is that more flexible exchange rates will lead to greater fluctuations of already unstable commodity prices. To

---

plier A's price index over four years is: 1.0, 0.9, 1.1, and 1.0. The index for supplier B is 1.0, 1.1, 0.9, and 1.0. (Deflation alternates with inflation, for simplicity.) In each year the LDC imports one physical unit from each supplier. The total cost in SDRs is precisely the same under fixed or floating rates, 8.0 SDRs; that is, under fixed rates, imports cost 1.0, 0.9, 1.1, and 1.0 from A and 1.0, 1.1, 0.9, and 1.0 from B. But under a floating regime, country A's currency in the second year is worth 1.1 SDRs while country B's is worth only 0.9; in the third year country A's currency falls 0.9 SDR and country B's rises to 1.1; in the fourth year the initial parities are reestablished. Thus under a float imports from A cost 1.0, 1.0, 1.0, and 1.0 SDR for the four consecutive years, as do those from B. That is, import cost in each year equals exchange rate multiplied by supplier's price stated in the supplier's domestic currency. Total cost is unchanged: floating has exactly replaced differential inflation. Indeed, under this complete "purchasing power parity exchange rate" specification, floating has reduced uncertainty by forcing to constancy the annual real cost of imports from each supplier. (I am indebted to Thomas D. Willett for clarification on this point.)

21. Reserves may also shift toward the LDCs from a developed country in deficit, although they will very probably be respent as soon as they are received.

put this argument in perspective it must be recognized that the magnitudes involved are not large.

For example, consider the sizable exchange rate realignments of December 1971 that led the LDCs as a group to experience approximately a 4 percent depreciation in rates vis-à-vis those of the industrial countries. This change was quite limited when compared to the actual price fluctuations of individual commodities attributable to specific supply and demand developments for each good.[22] Hence the purchasing power value of individual commodities would very probably be much more influenced by their specific supply and demand situations than by exchange rate fluctuations in a more flexible system. Such rate changes in any event would presumably be less pronounced than the Smithsonian realignment, which terminated a long period of frozen rates.

Much of the concern about the effects of flexible exchange rates on commodity price fluctuation appears to assume that the price of the good (say, coffee) in the currency of normal quotation (dollars) would remain unchanged even though the currency devalued, thereby imposing a real price decline on the commodity. Furthermore, some LDCs appear to have held the view that since many commodities are quoted in pounds or dollars, and since these two currencies in recent years have been expected to depreciate once greater flexibility were an option, real commodity prices would be bound to fall along with them. But this result has not occurred. Not only has the virulent commodity price inflation of 1973–74 (during a period of decline in these two currencies) belied this assumption, but the premise also fails to stand logical scrutiny. Suppose, for instance, that the dollar depreciates in terms of the franc; then if coffee is quoted in dollars its real price to the French declines, bidding up French demand; this increase in French demand boosts the dollar price, producing a price movement offsetting the depreciation of the dollar.[23]

22. For example, during 1972, selected dollar price changes were: cocoa, 19 percent; coffee, 12 percent; copper, −1 percent; cotton, 6 percent; fishmeal, 43 percent; rice, 13 percent; rubber, no change; sugar, 13 percent; tea, no change; tin, 8 percent. Changes in 1973 and 1974 were even larger. (Calculated from International Monetary Fund, *International Financial Statistics* [IMF, selected issues].)

23. This conclusion holds even if the price elasticity of demand is low. For example, an initial fall in the franc price of coffee after a depreciation of the dollar might generate little increased French consumption of coffee. But even when this small increase would require a bidding away of coffee from American consumers, who (by virtue of the same inelastic demand) would be prepared to pay substantially higher dollar prices to try to maintain their share of coffee supply. The result would be a rise in the dollar price.

Even the presence of a cartel should not change this effect. Suppose producers cooperate to maintain a dollar price at a level above competitive equilibrium but that maximizes revenue for the oligopoly of exporters. Then in the face of a dollar devaluation, there is no reason to expect the "real" monopoly profit potential of the cartel to decline, so that the producers should be able to raise the dollar price quotation sufficiently to offset the dollar's decline.[24]

THE FEAR that exchange rate flexibility will exacerbate the fluctuations of real commodity prices appears to have little theoretical justification. Fears that most commodity prices would sink by virtue of the millstone of their quotation in sinking dollars and pounds have been dramatically contradicted by recent commodity price explosions (even after taking into account the partial retreat of commodity prices since mid-1974).

Currency Bloc Problems

Most observers appear to assume that in a system with flexible rates among industrial countries, each LDC is likely to peg its own currency to that of one of the developed countries. Such a practice could give rise to five types of problems: (1) An LDC could be forced, by movements in the currency to which it is pegged—the "center currency"—to make appreciations or depreciations of its own currency vis-à-vis the rest of the world that might be inappropriate to its own balance of payments situation. (2) Choosing the center currency would involve difficult political decisions for each LDC on the "periphery." (3) Pegging to a center currency would frustrate LDC efforts to diversify trade among new partners because of the greater exchange rate risk involved in exporting to countries other than the one to which its currency is pegged. (4) LDC attempts at economic integration would be frustrated if prospective members are pegged to different center currencies. (5) Under the assumption that LDCs would peg to center currencies, greater flexibility would tend to divide the world into trading blocs.[25]

24. If over time the Organization of Petroleum Exporting Countries fails to raise the dollar price of oil to offset inflation, the implication will be that the real monopoly profit-maximizing price is falling (due to the greater need to discourage alternate supply as time passes), or else that noneconomic factors are constraining further increases.

25. These arguments about the problems associated with currency blocs are stressed by the Inter-American Committee on the Alliance for Progress (CIAP) in

Data are presented below indicating that floating beginning in 1973 did not lead to the formation of currency blocs of important magnitudes; LDCs in franc or sterling blocs accounted for a very minor portion of trade. Almost all the currencies of other LDCs were pegged to the dollar formally or informally (that is, pegged to the SDR, which until June 1974 was pegged to the dollar) or were following flexible rate practices themselves. Initial experience therefore contradicts the feared scenario of the trading world dividing up into major center-periphery blocs.

In an LDC's policy decision on exchange rate pegging practice, there are two obvious alternatives to simply pegging to the currency of the principal trading partner. First, and ideally, an LDC in a world of flexible rates could seek to maintain a target trade-weighted exchange rate. Thus, if the LDC wishes to avoid inappropriate depreciation, or appreciation, despite the fact that its principal industrial trading partner is depreciating, or appreciating, its monetary authorities should follow an intervention policy in which the change in the LDC's exchange rate would equal the trade-weighted average of exchange rate changes of all its major trading partners. Thus

$$(2) \qquad\qquad \dot{r}_{LDC} = \sum_i \lambda_i \, \dot{r}_i$$

where $\dot{r}_{LDC}$ is the percentage change in the LDC's exchange rate, $\dot{r}_i$ is the percentage change in the exchange rate of the major trading partner i, and λ_i is the trade share (for example, imports plus exports) of partner i in the LDC's trade.[26]

It would be possible to make this approach more precise if the LDC had reliable knowledge of its trade elasticities with each partner. The appropriate exchange movement would then be a function of trade-weighted partner exchange rate moves, with the weights adjusted to account for differing elasticities. Moreover, account could also be taken of financial

---

Latin America and the Reform of the International Monetary System (Washington, D.C.: Organization of American States, 1972), p. 49; Alexandre Kafka in *The I.M.F.: The Second Coming?* Essays in International Finance 94 (Princeton University, International Finance Section, 1972), p. 35; and Witteveen in IMF, *Summary Proceedings* (1973), p. 21.

26. For example, suppose the country conducts 50 percent of its trade with the United States and 50 percent with Germany. Suppose the mark appreciates by 20 percent vis-à-vis the dollar. Then the LDC currency (say, the peso) should appreciate vis-à-vis the dollar by 10 percent, which is arrived at as follows: $10 = (0.5 \times 0) + (0.5 \times 20)$.

flows and existing debt in addition to trade flows in establishing the appropriate weighting for the peg.[27]

A second basic alternative for the LDC would be to peg its currency not to a mother currency but to some international standard. Some LDCs have essentially chosen this option by pegging to the SDR. As constituted until mid-1974, the SDR was in a straitjacket with the dollar except in the instance of a specifically declared dollar devaluation (or revaluation) vis-à-vis the SDR (as in December 1971 and February 1973). This second option was therefore greatly improved in June 1974 when the SDR was redefined to be a "basket" of major currencies.[28] It seems very likely that in the future more LDCs will choose to peg to this more broadly based international unit of value, reducing or eliminating most of the problems anticipated by analysts if currency blocs are formed with LDCs pegging to a number of center currencies. Technically, the procedure of trade- and elasticity-weighted exchange rate variation described above would be superior to the option of pegging to SDRs consisting of a basket of currencies (because the weights of currencies in the basket may have little to do with trade weights of a particular LDC), but for operational simplicity pegging to the new SDR might be preferred.

FLEXIBLE EXCHANGE RATES among industrial countries are not likely to adversely affect world trade—and LDCs—because of the possible proliferation of currency blocs. In any event, an LDC has other choices that will

27. The optimal peg weighting scheme resulting from these various considerations is a subject requiring new analytical work. Note that Black has attempted to assess optimal LDC pegging strategy; he concludes that, if the objective is to minimize domestic price variance imposed by exchange rate fluctuations among other countries, the appropriate peg is a trade-weighted exchange rate, although adjustment in the rule is necessary depending on the covariance among exchange rates of major trading partners. (See Stanley W. Black, "Exchange Policies for Less Developed Countries in a World of Floating Rates," in D. M. Leipziger, ed., *The International Monetary System and the Developing Countries,* Proceedings of a conference held in Washington, D.C., June 4, 1975 [U.S. Agency for International Development; forthcoming].) Note that the study does not directly address the influence of debt composition on optimal pegging practice.

28. On June 13, 1974, the IMF executive directors adopted a redefinition of the SDR giving the following percentage weights to the sixteen currencies included in the basket: United States, 33 percent; Germany, 12½ percent; United Kingdom, 9 percent; France, 7½ percent; Japan, 7½ percent; Canada, 6 percent; Italy, 6 percent; Netherlands, 4½ percent; Belgium, 3½ percent; Sweden, 2½ percent; Australia, 1½ percent; Denmark, 1½ percent; Norway, 1½ percent; Spain, 1½ percent; Austria, 1 percent; South Africa, 1 percent. (*International Monetary Fund Survey,* June 17, 1974, p. 185.)

usually be superior to pegging its currency to that of its single major trading partner. And at least one of these (pegging to basket SDRs) will probably become increasingly popular.

Optimal Currency Area Arguments

The theory of optimal currency areas has been used in support of the notion that flexible exchange rates among developed countries would be disadvantageous to the LDCs. The argument runs thus: a small LDC must peg its currency to that of its major trading partner in order to obtain some of the benefits of an optimal currency area. The main benefit derived is the increased usefulness of its money, given the broader range of goods and services over which it then has command.[29] This gain is called an "intermediation" benefit by Mundell, who states that it confers a greater degree of "moneyness" on the currency.[30] If flexible rates are adopted by industrial countries, an LDC attempting to obtain optimal currency area benefits by pegging its currency to that of its chief trading partner will experience the difficulties discussed above. The particular problem of inappropriate shifts in exchange rate of the partner country vis-à-vis third countries will increase the reserve needs of the LDC. According to the argument, this effect will be more pronounced for LDCs than for industrial countries, since the latter are not so dependent on pegging their rates to those of partners because they themselves are closer to being "optimal currency areas" than are LDCs. As a result, there will be an increase in the reserve requirements of LDCs relative to those of industrial countries, and therefore grounds for "compensation" to LDCs for any monetary reform that involves more flexible rates for industrial countries. The quotas allocated to the LDCs by the International Monetary Fund should increase to reflect their greater relative need for reserves, or else the creation of SDRs should be linked to development assistance.[31]

29. Harry G. Johnson, "The Case for Flexible Exchange Rates, 1969," in George N. Halm, ed., *Approaches to Greater Flexibility of Exchange Rates: The Bürgenstock Papers* (Princeton University Press, 1970), p. 97.

30. Robert A. Mundell, "Uncommon Arguments for Common Currencies," in Harry G. Johnson and Alexander K. Swoboda, eds., *The Economics of Common Currencies: Proceedings of the Madrid Conference on Optimum Currency Areas* (London: Allen and Unwin, 1973), p. 128.

31. For an explicit statement of this line of argument, see Carlos F. Díaz-Alejandro, *Less Developed Countries and the Post-1971 International Financial System,* Essays in International Finance 108 (Princeton University, International Finance Section, 1975).

The practical value of the optimal currency area theory in this connection seems limited. As a general matter this theory has remained unfortunately devoid of quantification of costs, such as the loss of domestic policy autonomy, relative to benefits.[32] With regard to the point at hand, it is unclear that the psychological benefit of increasing the "usefulness" or "moneyness" of the small LDC's currency by pegging to one partner's currency outweighs the cost of surrender of autonomy in domestic policy. Indeed, Kenen argues quite the contrary—that countries with little diversification in their economies and exports should employ more exchange rate flexibility than large, diversified economies that are much more capable of absorbing external shocks without having to change their exchange rates.[33]

Of the various hypothesized benefits of optimal currency areas, a principal architect of the theory stresses the savings in reserve requirements that may be achieved through pooling of all members' reserves in a currency union.[34] This benefit is irrelevant to a pseudo currency union in which a small LDC pegs its currency to that of a major partner but the two engage in no such formal arrangements as reserve pooling.

THE THEORY of the optimal currency area appears to warrant little weight in the argument that LDCs would be disadvantaged by more flexible rates for the industrial countries.

Reserve Management

Flexibility of exchange rates among industrial countries adds to the complexity of reserve management for LDCs; countries must take into

32. See the excellent survey by Yoshihide Ishiyama, "The Theory of Optimum Currency Areas: A Survey," in International Monetary Fund, *Staff Papers,* vol. 22, no. 2 (IMF, July 1975), pp. 344–83. Also note the plea for more empirical research in the field by Edward Tower and Thomas Willett, in "The Theory of Optimum Currency Areas and Exchange Rate Flexibility: A More General Framework." (Department of the Treasury, Office of the Assistant Secretary of the Treasury for International Affairs, Discussion Paper Series [1975; processed].)

33. Kenen states: "The less-developed countries, being less diversified and less well-equipped with policy instruments, should make more frequent changes or perhaps resort to full flexibility." (Peter Kenen, "The Theory of Optimum Currency Areas: An Eclectic View," in Robert A. Mundell and Alexander K. Swoboda, eds., *Monetary Problems of the International Economy* [University of Chicago Press, 1969], p. 54.)

34. Robert A. Mundell, "Uncommon Arguments for Common Currencies," in Johnson and Swoboda, eds., *Common Currencies,* pp. 114–32.

account the risk of exchange realignment in their choice of reserve assets.[35] One issue is whether more flexible rates would reduce the need for reserves and thereby permit social savings to the extent that the opportunity cost of capital (or foreign exchange) exceeds the interest earned on the reserve asset. In a system of exchange rates that are fixed for developed but flexible for less developed countries, savings from reduced reserves would be a distinct possibility.[36] However, flexible rates for industrial countries might well increase LDC reserve requirements because of new needs to provide for temporary fluctuations in the real value of foreign exchange earnings.

Aside from the decision on the level of reserves, decisions on their composition would also be affected by greater flexibility. A reasonable principle to apply would be to hold a balanced portfolio of foreign currency assets as foreign exchange reserves.[37] This balance could be related to the shares of various industrial countries in the LDC's imports, as well as to the proportionate mix of foreign currencies in which debt service obligations are denominated.[38]

35. The dangers are dramatically illustrated by the statement of the spokesman for Gambia at the 1973 IMF and World Bank annual meetings: "Despite the guarantee provided by the Sterling Agreement, the downward floating of the pound, combined with the two devaluations of the dollar, has led to a reserve loss that, in real terms, is equivalent to some 5 per cent of the Gambia's gross domestic product." (I. M. Garba-Jahumpa, "Discussion of Fund Policy at Third Joint Session," in IMF, *Summary Proceedings* [1973], p. 97.)

36. As emphasized by A. Roberto Campos, "Observations," in CIAP, *Latin America and the Reform of the International Monetary System*, p. 83.

37. Countries that were risk-takers might choose to concentrate their reserves in currencies expected to appreciate.

38. Note that Haberler's warning against the inflationary impact of various countries' holding several other countries' currencies as reserves does not apply to this recommendation for LDC portfolio diversification. (See Gottfried Haberler, *Two Essays on the Future of the International Monetary Order*.) In the standard case, if industrial country *A* holds *B*'s currency and *B* returns the favor, each one expands its own domestic money supply by the money multiplier applied to the increase in money base from new "reserves." A seemingly harmless swap thus creates pressure toward monetary expansion in both. However, LDCs beginning to hold marks or francs would merely be switching them for dollars originally held. The total of foreign currency reserves would therefore not rise. (This assumes that the dollars were sold for marks in the private exchange market; Germany's reserves, in this example, would rise if, instead, the German government purchased the dollars to avoid appreciation.) It is true that portfolio diversification would tend to accentuate pressures on rates, because LDCs would bid up the price of strong currencies even further as they moved into them, while bidding down the price of dollars by increasing the supply for sale.

Empirical evidence on the extent of LDC foreign exchange reserve composition is not publicly available. However, of $16 billion held by LDCs in foreign exchange reserves in mid-1971, only $6 billion could be positively attributed to dollar and sterling assets on the basis of U.S. and British financial statistics.[39] Part of the $10 billion difference probably consisted of LDC dollar holdings in the Eurodollar market, but the discrepancy indicates that there may already exist substantially more portfolio diversification than is commonly assumed, and this tendency must have increased since mid-1971.

A more satisfactory solution than diversification of foreign exchange holdings would be to make available an international asset such as the new SDR consisting of a basket of currencies, but with the additional advantage that it could be actively purchased and sold.[40] With such a revised SDR mechanism, countries could sell foreign exchange to purchase basket SDRs directly from other holders. This process admittedly would lead to downward pressure on those currencies that were already weak, since other countries would attempt to move their reserves away from these currencies into SDRs or other currencies.

Finally, it must be emphasized that the increased risk of holding foreign exchange reserves in a system of flexible rates cannot be criticized without taking into account the offsetting factor that such assets yield higher interest return than gold or the SDR (even after the increase in the SDR's interest rate from 1½ percent to 5 percent in mid-1974).

FLEXIBILITY OF EXCHANGE RATES among industrial countries may add to the complexities of LDC reserve management. Increased risk of changing real value of foreign exchange reserves can be moderated by the diversification of currencies or by the holding of SDRs. In any event, the real risk of holding foreign exchange reserves will be greater under a fixed-rate system than in a flexible-rate system if, as seems likely, the fixed rates finally collapse in large, rending readjustments after prolonged periods,

39. Gerald K. Helleiner, "The Less Developed Countries and the International Monetary System," *Journal of Development Studies,* vol. 10 (April–July 1974), p. 355.

40. At present all SDR transactions are through the IMF, and a transaction arises only when a holder of SDRs wishes to "use" them for balance settlement; the IMF accepts the SDRs and then transfers them to the account of another country, which pays for them with its own convertible currency or with another reserve asset. Active purchase of SDRs is impossible under the present system.

whereas flexible rates move much more moderately though more frequently.

Problems for Debt Management

Flexible exchange rates among developed countries may change the real value of foreign debt contracted by LDCs. In the 1971 and 1973 dollar devaluations, LDCs with debt denominated in yen or European currencies suffered losses, but these losses were much more than offset by windfall gains caused by the decline in the real value of dollar-denominated debt (as discussed below).

A major consideration is the erosion of the real debt burden by ongoing inflation in the creditor country, quite apart from exchange realignment. Recent inflation rates have made even "hard-term" loans to LDCs practically free of real cost. However, exchange rate movements under a more flexible system would partially substitute for differential inflation rates among developed countries. One risk, in fact, would be substituted for another.

With respect to debt management, LDCs could lessen prospective shocks from rate realignments by contracting their debt among industrial creditor countries in proportions similar to those of their export trade shares. The result would be that an increased real debt service burden on the portion of debt held by an industrial country with an appreciating currency would tend to be covered by increased earnings of export sales to that country because, if an LDC's currency depreciated relative to that of the developed country, there should be a proportionate increase in LDC sales to that country operating on an original trade base proportional to the latter's weight in the debt portfolio.

Predictions of specific "injuries" to the capital market have been made. Mundell, for instance, has argued that flexible rates among developed countries will increase the cost of capital to LDCs, because potential lenders will demand higher-risk premiums in their decisions to lend abroad to cover greater exchange risk.[41] It would seem that the validity of this argument once again hinges on whether increased frequency of rate changes will lessen magnitudes of shifts sufficiently to reduce, rather than

41. Robert A. Mundell, "The International Monetary System and Development Finance," Paper presented to the Intergovernmental Group of Seventy-seven on International Monetary Matters by the Delegation of Mexico (1972; processed).

raise, overall exchange rate uncertainty of a flexible system compared to a fixed-rate system.

Kafka has argued that flexible exchange rates would permit national policymakers to pursue more independent interest rate policies and that the resulting increase in interest rate fluctuations would mean greater uncertainty for LDCs in their borrowing on world capital markets.[42] This argument is less than convincing. First, large portions of LDC borrowings are from institutions notorious for maintaining constant interest rates despite market rate conditions (the multilateral lending agencies and the official export credit agencies of advanced countries). Second, one could just as easily argue that LDCs could take advantage of greater interest rate fluctuations among developed countries by borrowing from the cheapest source at any given time, profiting from the temporary existence of lower interest rates in individual markets caused by greater monetary independence (given the original assumption by Kafka of greater independence with flexible rates).[43]

Finally, one institutional difficulty of debt management under exchange rate flexibility for industrial countries is that international lending agencies' loans are denominated in whatever currency the agency happens to have available, meaning that one LDC may receive a loan in marks and another in dollars. This practice could easily be revised to mix currencies in loan denominations so as to spread the risk of changing real value of debt burden due to exchange rate realignment among industrial countries.

WITH APPROPRIATE POLICIES of debt management, such as diversification of the currency of denomination for debt, LDCs should be able to minimize fluctuations in the real burden of debt caused by flexible rates among industrial countries.

Scarcity of Expertise

One argument frequently made is that LDCs are at a disadvantage in a more flexible exchange rate system due to their scarcity of expertise.

42. Alexandre Kafka, *"The I.M.F.: The Second Coming?"*
43. Furthermore, the more conventional view than that proposed by Kafka is that exchange rate policy and monetary policy tend to be substitutes; that under fixed rates, changing monetary policy (and hence changing interest rates) must be used to achieve foreign balance. Thus, the standard interpretation would be that interest rates would be more stable under flexible than under fixed rates.

Skilled personnel are required to deal with the great increase in a need for frequent decisions on reserve and debt management in the face of changing rates among industrial countries, and to take the crucial decisions regarding the appropriate exchange rate response to these changes.

Ironically, a former planning minister of Brazil has argued just the opposite with respect to flexibility for an LDC's own exchange rate:

> In a developing country, where managerial skill is a highly scarce commodity, rate flexibility accomplished automatically and effectively what administratively is highly difficult and time consuming to do. Where there is a shortage of external resources, a mini-devaluation can allocate scarce foreign exchange, or grant export subsidies, much more quickly, equitably and more efficiently than administrative action.[44]

CONCERNING THE INDIRECT EFFECTS of flexible rates among developed countries, it seems indisputable that more frequent technical decisions would be required for LDCs than under a fixed-rate system. In practice, most LDCs appear to be taking the line of least resistance by merely pegging to the dollar or the SDR. The discussion above suggests that more sophisticated exchange policies would be preferable. One solution to the problem of expertise scarcity would be to extend the consultant services of the International Monetary Fund.

Forward Exchange Markets; Terms of Trade

The 1973 IMF annual report specifically cited forward exchange market development as a major new cost that LDCs would have to bear under a system of flexible rates for industrial countries.[45] However, the importance of this problem seems to have been exaggerated. Most LDC export and import contracts have traditionally been specified in the major foreign currencies, not in a local currency. To the extent that LDC traders wished to hedge against new relative movements of these foreign currencies, they could do so through established forward exchange markets in the financial centers of industrial countries. The absence in LDCs of forward exchange markets for this purpose therefore appears to be of little concern.

44. A. Roberto Campos, "Observations," in CIAP, *Latin America*, p. 83.
45. International Monetary Fund, *Annual Report of the Executive Directors for the Fiscal Year Ended April 30, 1973* (IMF, 1973), p. 32.

When it is important to have local currency quotations for certain export and import contracts, the problem is one of forward cover not among currencies of developed countries but between a specific foreign currency and the domestic currency of the LDC. In this case new forward markets would undoubtedly be required; but it would seem they could be provided fairly simply. The reason is that most LDC exchange rates are overvalued, so that it would impose little expected cost on an LDC's central bank to guarantee, say, the current peso-dollar (or peso-SDR) rate for, say, six months to future recipients of dollars. There would be no anticipation of peso appreciation so the central bank would not suffer loss. Once the forward market for pesos to dollars existed, the trader could then complete his coverage by using forward markets of the major foreign financial centers to convert to dollars from the currency in which payment was to be received.

The above process would provide a low-cost forward cover to LDC exporters but not to LDC importers, because the central bank concerned would be wise to buy dollars forward but foolish to sell them forward in the face of possible peso depreciation. However, to the extent that absence of forward cover for imports diminished importation, the pressure on scarce foreign exchange would be relieved and, if the LDC wished to stimulate imports, a more efficient way than the provision of forward exchange cover would probably be a compensating reduction in tariffs, quotas, and other import restrictions prevalent in LDCs.[46]

Another typical LDC fear appears to be that terms of trade of developing countries would deteriorate as a result of more flexible rates among industrial countries. The implicit assumptions are that the dollar and pound are likely to depreciate, that many commodity prices are quoted in one or the other, and that these quotations would not rise enough to offset declines in currency values. As argued above, this assumption has no theoretical basis. Furthermore, it is contradicted by recent experience. LDC terms of trade have improved enormously during a time of—though not necessarily because of—floating rates. (There is, in fact, a large net

46. India has adopted precisely the one-sided type of forward exchange facility proposed here. Beginning in June 1974, the Indian government offered forward exchange guarantee to exporters of capital goods with anticipated payment in the future (eighteen months to ten years) accruing in pounds sterling, U.S. dollars, deutsche marks, or Japanese yen. (Reserve Bank of India, Exchange Control Department, "Provision of Long-Term Forward Exchange Cover to Exporters in Respect of Exports Made on Deferred Payment Terms" [May 25, 1974; processed].)

improvement remaining despite a partial backing off of commodity prices since mid-1974.)

Little more needs to be said about terms of trade beyond what has already been discussed. However, it is useful to dispel one misunderstanding. When the dollar, for example, depreciates by 10 percent vis-à-vis all other currencies, it is not necessary for the dollar price of, say, coffee to rise a full 10 percent to hold terms of trade constant. The reason is that the LDC imports a significant portion of its goods from the United States, and for this fraction of its imports there need be no increase in the coffee export price whatsoever to maintain constant terms of trade.

THE ARGUMENT that flexible rates among industrial countries would impose forward exchange costs on LDCs cannot be faulted in terms of direction; in terms of magnitude, however, it appears of only limited significance. In relation to terms of trade, the fears of adverse effects have little theoretical foundation and have not been realized in practice.

Share in the Gains for the World Economy

The most important effects of flexible rates among developed countries will not be the direct effects on LDCs enumerated above, but rather the indirect effect of overall improvement or deterioration in the world trading and financial system, in comparison with results under fixed rates. Given the magnitude of foreign exchange receipts from exports and capital inflows ($140 billion in 1973), it would take only minor improvements in the world trading and monetary system through the introduction of flexible rates to completely offset any likely losses incurred by LDCs for reasons such as those cited above. For example, the IMF estimates that the Smithsonian realignment caused a loss of real reserve value for the LDCs of $500 million. Even ignoring the offsetting decline in real value of LDC foreign debt, this loss would be fully offset by only a small percentage increase in overall trade and capital flows stemming from an improved exchange rate regime.[47]

The interests of the LDCs in monetary reform lie overwhelmingly with those of the industrial countries. If greater exchange rate flexibility will

---

47. Assuming a typical LDC shadow price of foreign exchange of 1.33 in relation to a market rate of 1.00, it would require an increase in LDC exchange earnings of only one percentage point to offset a $500 million windfall reserve loss.

improve the overall trading and capital flow system, both will benefit; if departure from fixed rates will injure the system, both will lose. The losses peculiar to LDCs caused by greater flexibility should be very minor indeed compared with the gains or losses they can expect from participating in the improvement or deterioration of the system as a whole.

Empirical Evidence

The robust trade performance of developing countries since the major currencies began to float has contradicted the expectation of injury to the LDCs from a system of flexible rates. Losses in real value of dollar reserves held by LDCs have been minor and have been offset by gains from the reduced real burden of dollar-denominated debt.

Trade Performance

If flexible exchange rates among developed countries are considered detrimental to LDCs, then LDC export growth would have been expected to suffer and its relative importance to decrease in 1972 after the Smithsonian realignment of exchange rates among the industrial nations, and to decline still more beginning in 1973 when industrial countries' currencies started floating. Table 2-2 presents data on exports in the period 1967–74 for both industrial and less developed countries. Between 1967 and 1971 exports from developing countries, excluding oil exporters, grew somewhat more slowly than those from industrial countries; the average growth rate of the former over these years was less than four-fifths the rate of the latter. The relationship reversed in 1972: LDC exports grew faster than those of advanced countries, contrary to the hypothesis that they were injured by the Smithsonian changes. During 1973 and 1974 dollar export values mushroomed by enormous proportions for all countries. LDC growth was once again greater than that of industrial nations, and the export growth of oil-exporting countries, of course, grew by much greater proportions.

Because of a massive commodity price explosion in 1973 and 1974, attributable in substantial measure to factors other than floating rates (particularly simultaneous booms in the industrial countries), LDC export growth was larger than usual in these years. To help isolate the influence of exchange rate regimes, table 2-2 also reports the growth of

Table 2-2. *Export Growth of Industrial and Developing Countries, 1967–74*
Amounts in billions of dollars

	Industrial countries and other developed areas		Oil-exporting countries		Developing countries excluding oil-exporting countries		Manufactured exports of twenty developing countries[a]	
	Exports (1)	*Percent growth* (2)	*Exports* (3)	*Percent growth* (4)	*Exports* (5)	*Percent growth* (6)	*Amount* (7)	*Percent growth* (8)
1967	151.2	...	13.2	...	26.2	...	n.a.	...
1968	169.9	12.4	14.8	12.1	28.5	8.8	n.a.	...
1969	196.1	15.4	16.1	8.8	32.5	14.0	4.61	...
1970	226.2	15.3	18.3	13.7	36.2	11.4	5.47	18.7
1971	252.8	11.8	24.2	32.2	37.8	4.4	6.42	17.5
1972	300.5	18.9	29.1	20.2	45.1	19.3	8.44	31.4
1973	410.6	36.6	43.6	80.9	65.5	45.2	n.a.	...
1974	544.9	32.7	136.9[b]	214.0	93.7[b]	43.0	n.a.	...

Sources: Columns 1 through 6, calculated from International Monetary Fund, *International Financial Statistics*, vol. 28 (April 1975); columns 7 and 8, calculated from United Nations, *Yearbook of International Trade Statistics, 1972–1973* (United Nations, 1974). (Country categories in columns 1 through 6 as defined in *International Financial Statistics*.)
n.a. Not available.
a. Standard international trade classification categories 5 to 8 for Brazil, Egypt, Ghana, Hong Kong, Iran, Iraq, Kenya, Korea, Mexico, Nigeria, Pakistan, Singapore, Sudan, Syria, Tanzania, Thailand, Trinidad and Tobago, Turkey, Uganda, and Uruguay.
b. Estimated.

manufactured exports for twenty of the major developing countries for which data are available. The ratio of the growth rate of these LDC manufactured exports to the growth rate of total exports of industrial countries indicates a strong upsurge in LDC exports in 1972 rather than any deterioration. (Comparable data for 1973 and 1974 were not available in November 1975.) Of course, the underlying growth rate of these manufactured exports was already high, because of expansion from such a low base and because of aggressive new industrial export schemes in several LDCs; the acceleration in 1972 could hardly be ascribed to a new climate in world exchange regimes. However, the point remains that these data contradict rather than support the notion that the Smithsonian realignment of exchange rates discouraged LDC exports by raising exchange rate uncertainty.

Two beneficial effects of the Smithsonian realignment of exchange rates and of floating beginning in 1973 are worth noting. First, by pegging to the dollar in the 1971 and 1973 devaluations, many developing countries took the opportunity to devalue and thereby presumably stimulated their exports to higher levels than would have been possible without devaluation. Second, a side effect of the 1973 floating regime may have been to boost commodity prices as speculators left currencies in general to purchase gold and other commodities. From their 1972 weighted average, the dollar prices of twenty-three of the commodity exports most important to LDCs (excluding oil) rose by 120 percent to a peak in the second quarter of 1974.[48] Factors other than the floating of exchange rates were undoubtedly primarily responsible—including a convergence of cyclical upswings in the industrial economies during the year, and a general flight from money into goods associated with accelerating inflation—but at least some portion of the commodity price explosion may have been due to portfolio diversification away from currency into goods because of the floating of exchange rates and a resulting increase in the perceived risk of holding currencies.[49]

48. Calculated from the International Monetary Fund, *International Financial Statistics* (IMF, selected issues). By September 1974 the average price of the same group of commodities was 80 percent above the 1972 level, whereas in 1973 it was only 55 percent above the 1972 level.

49. Note further that dollar devaluation per se does not seem to have been the major source of the dollar price rise in commodities. Thus in 1972 the dollar price of these same commodities rose by only 8 percent following the Smithsonian devaluation. The much larger 1973 price rises followed a dollar devaluation of approximately the same magnitude as the Smithsonian devaluation.

Effects of Dollar Devaluations

Following the Smithsonian realignment of exchange rates there was considerable publicity about its effects on the developing countries. At UNCTAD III in 1972, LDC participants drafted resolutions that charged damage from loss of dollar reserve value and deterioration in terms of trade, and they demanded compensation.

Despite these claims, there were both positive and negative effects for the LDCs resulting from the December 1971 and February 1973 dollar devaluations.

The positive effects included: (1) an increase in the real value of LDCs' reserves held in gold or in appreciating foreign currencies; (2) a decrease in the real value of outstanding foreign debt denominated in dollars; (3) a probable rise in the dollar quotations of commodity prices following upon the supply and demand reaction to the initial decline in the real price of commodities traded with dollar price quotations; and (4) the expectation that the effective devaluation by the many LDCs maintaining parity with the devalued dollar would stimulate their exports, reduce their imports, and relax foreign exchange constraints on their domestic growth.

The negative effects were: (1) reserves held in dollars lost purchasing power; (2) the real cost of the repayment burden of debt denominated in appreciating currencies, such as the yen and deutsche mark, increased; and (3) imports from countries with appreciating currencies became more expensive in terms of the dollars earned by LDCs.

The IMF has estimated several of these effects for both of the dollar devaluations. Although details of these calculations are not publicly available, the results, presented in table 2-3, appear to be reasonable. The estimates imply that the LDCs were not on balance injured by the dollar devaluations. Their gains through reduction in real value of foreign debt offset their losses through decline in purchasing power of dollar reserves.[50] Furthermore, the IMF predictions of improved trade balances were at least consistent with the strong export performance of the LDCs in 1972 and 1973. It is true that LDC terms of trade deteriorated slightly as a result of the devaluation (that is, devaluation partially dampened com-

50. According to the IMF, each effect was approximately $500 million. Since the February 1973 results showed a smaller percentage decline in real reserves and a larger percentage decline in real debt than occurred in the first devaluation, the net result was presumably favorable rather than nil.

Table 2-3. *Economic Effects of the 1971 and 1973 Dollar Devaluations on Selected Economic Variables for Less Developed Countries*
Percent

Effect	December 1971	February 1973
Average appreciation of LDC currencies vis-à-vis the dollar	4.0	5.0
Average depreciation of LDC currencies relative to those of all industrial countries	4.5	2.0
Deterioration in terms of trade	1.0[a]	0.5[a]
Induced average rise in U.S. dollar prices of LDC exports and imports	7.4	7.0
Rise in dollar value of LDC reserves	5.0	5.0
Decline in purchasing power of LDC reserves	2.3[b]	2.0
Rise in dollar value of debt		
All LDCs	4.5–5.0	5.0
Africa	n.a.	6.5
Latin America	n.a.	4.0
Decline in real value of debt	1.0–1.5[b]	1.5–2.0
Probable induced change		
In import volume	−2.0[a]	−1.0[a]
In export volume	1.5–2.0[a]	1.0[a]
In trade balance	...[a,c]	...[a,d]

Sources: International Monetary Fund, *Annual Report of the Executive Directors for the Fiscal Year Ended April 30, 1973* (IMF, 1973), pp. 29–31; *Annual Report* (1972), pp. 22–23.
a. Hypothetical calculations requiring elasticity assumptions.
b. Approximately $500 million.
c. $1.5 billion to $2 billion.
d. $1 billion.

modity price rises, according to the IMF calculations). However, that result in part reflected the countries' own decision to devalue and to stimulate their trade balances. There will typically be welfare gains for the developing country resulting from trade balance improvement, because the scarcity value of foreign exchange to its national product usually exceeds that indicated by the market exchange rate. Moreover, increased exports afford the opportunity for increased utilization of underemployed labor in an LDC as well as the increased exploitation of economies of scale. Therefore, it is possible and even likely for these welfare gains to have more than offset the welfare loss from any terms of trade deterioration associated with dollar devaluations.

A GOOD CASE can be made that the two dollar devaluations benefited rather than injured the LDCs. The effective devaluation should have had a beneficial impact on LDC trade balances and foreign exchange constraints, whereas the two direct effects of reserve loss and real debt reduction canceled out each other. The aggregate results reported here mask regional variations. Individual countries suffered more, the more their exports were channeled to dollar area countries, their imports drawn from appreciating countries, their debt denominated in nondollar currencies, and their reserves held in dollars. Asian countries importing from Japan but exporting to the United States are likely to have benefited less or suffered more than Latin American countries importing more heavily from the United States, exporting to Europe, and having a larger portion of debt denominated in dollars.

LDC Pegging Practice

An important area for empirical examination is the currency pegging practices of the developing countries since the Smithsonian realignment of exchange rates in December 1971. This evidence is relevant to assess the concern that exchange rate flexibility will carve up the trading world into blocs, with the danger of eventual reduction in trade outside the blocs as well as the more immediate difficulty of exchange rate movements in the "center" of each bloc not necessarily appropriate to the situations of its "periphery" countries. Table 2-4 reports the pegging practices of sixty-one developing countries (with populations of over 2 million), at the time of the Smithsonian realignment and as of July 1973 and June 1975. The following patterns emerge.

1. In response to the 1971 realignment, the French African countries tended to remain pegged to the franc, British Commonwealth countries to the pound, and most other LDCs to the dollar. There were, however, numerous countries that pegged to the dollar despite their traditional membership in franc or sterling areas: a reasonable response for the many LDCs with chronically overvalued exchange rates and political resistance to more direct devaluation measures. In the aggregate, LDCs remaining with the franc, pound, and gold represented 30 percent of total LDC import value of these sixty-one countries.[51] A group representing 41 percent

51. Note that table 2-4 includes countries representing only 74 percent of total LDC import value.

of import value remained at par with the dollar, while a third group of countries amounting to 29 percent of LDC import value adopted other responses, most of them devaluation beyond that of the dollar (but probably by lesser amounts than they would have devalued vis-à-vis the dollar had it not declined).

2. By mid-1973, the weight (by value of imports) of countries pegging to the dollar had considerably increased. Countries formally pegging to the pound and franc represented a total of only 8 percent of LDC import values, those with flexible rates 10 percent, those formally pegging to the dollar 51 percent,[52] and those pegging to the dollar de facto (by pegging to the SDR or gold) 31 percent. These figures cast serious doubt on the notion that several important currency blocs would form as a result of floating rates. By mid-1973 there were only minor franc and sterling LDC blocs, and no yen or deutsche mark blocs.[53]

3. The LDCs moving informally with the dollar in mid-1973 because they maintained a par value with the SDR represent a special case. Most of them appreciated vis-à-vis the dollar at the time of the February 1973 dollar devaluation (table 2-4, note b). Hence, it would be misleading to infer that they were strictly pegged to the dollar. Rather, they were tied to the SDR, which until June 1974 was specified in terms of a dollar parity (although this parity changed in each of the two dollar devaluations). As a result, in mid-1973 any currency maintaining parity with the SDR was in practice also tied to the dollar (except in the event of explicit devaluation of the dollar vis-à-vis the SDR) and floated with it against the other major currencies.

4. By mid-1975 many countries previously pegging to both the SDR and the dollar had been forced to choose between the two because of the divorce of the SDR from a dollar par in mid-1974. It is remarkable that the large majority of countries in this situation chose to peg to the dollar rather than to the SDR. Nineteen countries[54] with diverse geographical locations opted for the dollar, whereas only four countries[55] had moved to

52. However, 19 percent out of the 51 percent represented countries, such as Brazil and Colombia, which frequently adjusted their exchange rates although pegging to the dollar between adjustments. See table 2-4, note d.

53. Based on trade values. Given the pegging of India and Bangladesh to the pound, however, the "sterling bloc" was substantial in terms of LDC population.

54. Bolivia, Burundi, Republic of China, Dominican Republic, Ecuador, Ethiopia, Guinea, Haiti, Iraq, Kenya, Nepal, Pakistan, Rwanda, Tanzania, Thailand, Turkey, Uganda, Zaire, Zambia.

55. Burma, Iran, Malawi, Saudi Arabia.

Table 2-4. *Currency Pegging Practices of Sixty-one Developing Countries with Populations of over Two Million, 1971–75*

Country	Currency area (1)	1972 Imports (millions of dollars) (2)	December 1971 in response to Smithsonian realignment[a] (3)	As of July 16, 1973 (4)	As of June 30, 1975 (5)
Africa					
Algeria	franc	1,372	GFP	SDR[b]	flexible
Burundi	...	31	dollar	SDR[b]	dollar
Cameroon	franc	299	GFP	franc	franc
Chad	franc	n.a.	GFP	franc	franc
Egypt	...	877	dollar	dollar[b]	dollar
Ethiopia	...	189	GFP	SDR[b]	dollar
Ghana	...	431	devalued[c]	dollar[b]	dollar
Guinea	franc	n.a.	GFP	SDR[b]	dollar
Ivory Coàst	franc	447	GFP	franc	franc
Kenya	pound	560	dollar	SDR	dollar
Malagasy Republic	franc	213	GFP	franc	franc
Malawi	pound	130	GFP	pound	SDR
Mali	franc	70	GFP	franc	franc
Morocco	franc	766	GFP	flexible	flexible
Niger	franc	n.a.	GFP	franc	franc
Nigeria	pound	1,502	GFP	SDR	flexible
Rwanda	...	35	GFP	SDR[b]	dollar
Senegal	franc	276	GFP	franc	franc
Sudan	...	320	dollar	dollar	dollar
Tanzania, United Republic of	pound	406	dollar	SDR	dollar
Tunisia	franc	460	GFP	SDR[b]	flexible
Uganda	pound	250	dollar	SDR	dollar
Upper Volta	franc	n.a.	GFP	franc	franc
Zaire	...	643	dollar	SDR	dollar
Zambia	pound	718	dollar	SDR[b]	dollar
Latin America					
Argentina	dollar	1,868	dollar	dollar	dollar
Bolivia	dollar	185	dollar	SDR	dollar
Brazil	...	4,783	devalued[c]	dollar[d]	dollar[d]
Chile	...	980	devalued[c]	dollar	dollar
Colombia	...	836	devalued[c]	dollar[d]	dollar[d]
Dominican Republic	dollar	370	dollar	SDR	dollar
Ecuador	dollar	327	dollar	SDR	dollar
El Salvador	dollar	276	dollar	dollar	dollar
Guatemala	dollar	324	dollar	dollar	dollar
Haiti	dollar	64	dollar	SDR	dollar
Mexico	dollar	2,932	dollar	dollar	dollar
Peru	dollar	791	dollar	dollar	dollar
Venezuela	...	2,118	appreciated[c]	dollar	dollar
Asia					
Afghanistan	...	113	dollar	dollar	dollar
Bangladesh	...	n.a.	...	pound	pound
Burma	...	133	devalued[c]	SDR[b]	SDR
China, Republic of	...	1,844	dollar	SDR[b]	dollar
Hong Kong	pound	3,902	GFP	dollar	dollar
India	...	2,273	appreciated[c]	pound	pound
Iran	...	2,410	dollar	SDR[b]	SDR
Iraq	...	713	GFP	SDR[b]	dollar
Khmer Republic (Cambodia)	...	78	dollar	dollar[d]	flexible
Korea	...	2,522	flexible	dollar[d]	dollar[d]

Table 2-4 (*continued*)

Country	Currency area (1)	1972 Imports (millions of dollars) (2)	December 1971 in response to Smithsonian realignment[a] (3)	As of July 16, 1973 (4)	As of June 30, 1975 (5)
			Currency to which country pegged		
Malaysia	pound	1,638	GFP	flexible	flexible
Nepal	...	50	dollar	SDR	dollar
Pakistan	pound	705	GFP	SDR[b]	dollar
Philippines	dollar	1,366	dollar	dollar[d]	flexible
Saudi Arabia	...	806	GFP	SDR[b]	SDR
Sri Lanka	pound	342	dollar	pound	pound
Syria	...	477	dollar	dollar	dollar
Thailand	...	1,484	dollar	SDR	dollar
Vietnam, Republic of	...	707	dollar	dollar[d]	dollar[d]
Yemen Arab Republic	...	n.a.	flexible	flexible	dollar
Europe					
Turkey	...	1,558	appreciated[c]	SDR	dollar
Yugoslavia	...	3,233	GFP	flexible	flexible
Oceania					
Indonesia	...	1,458	dollar	dollar[d]	dollar[d]
Total		53,661			

Sources: Columns 1 and 3, Gerald K. Helleiner, "The Less Developed Countries and the International Monetary System," *Journal of Development Studies*, vol. 10 (April–July 1974), p. 359; column 4, Helleiner, ibid., p. 362, and International Monetary Fund, *Annual Report* (1973), pp. 70–73; column 2, International Monetary Fund, *International Financial Statistics*, selected issues; column 5, International Monetary Fund, *Annual Report* (1975), pp. 68–70.

n.a. Not available.

a. GFP indicates that a country maintained its currency at parity with gold, the franc, or the pound.

b. Currency appreciated vis-à-vis the dollar in the February 1973 dollar devaluation, despite subsequent pegging to the dollar or to the Special Drawing Right at parity with the dollar.

c. Movement of currency vis-à-vis the dollar at the time of the Smithsonian realignment of exchange rates.

d. Country frequently readjusts its exchange rate although its currency is pegged to the dollar between adjustments.

a peg to the SDR (and one of these, Malawi, had moved from the pound to the SDR rather than from the dollar). It would seem that for many of the countries that chose to peg to the dollar a more appropriate choice would have been the new basket SDR. Denominated as a weighted average of several currencies, the new SDR should give a currency peg that is closer to a trade-weighted "effective exchange rate" for most of the LDCs than the dollar alone, except for those countries that trade almost exclusively with the United States.[56] It is possible that as countries gain experience with floating among the major currencies and with the new SDR, more of them will move toward a peg to the SDR instead of to the dollar.

56. See page 25, note 28, for the currencies and proportions decided upon for the basket SDR in mid-1974.

5. Flexible exchange rates had been adopted by eight LDCs[57] by mid-1975 and another five[58] were frequently adjusting rates pegged to the dollar and therefore had characteristics similar to flexible rates. However, in the latter case, frequent adjustments were typically applied to offset rapid domestic inflation, so that exchange rate fluctuation did not represent floating with little government intervention and with both upward and downward oscillations in the real exchange rate.

6. By mid-1975, it had become even clearer that the LDCs did not group into currency blocs around the franc, pound, and dollar. Instead, they overwhelmingly opted for pegging to the dollar alone. Fully two-thirds of import value was accounted for by countries pegged to the dollar.[59] The only other widespread practice was the use of flexible rates, representing 19.4 percent of LDC import value. Of countries with populations of over two million, eight African countries remained tied to the franc, but their weight in LDC imports was a mere 2.4 percent; only India, Bangladesh, and Sri Lanka remained tied to the pound (accounting for only 5 percent of LDC imports); and the four countries pegged to the new SDR represented only 6.5 percent of LDC import value.

IN SUM, actual experience with floating rates among industrial countries has not borne out fears that the trading world would be carved up into franc, pound, and dollar blocs. However, the experience does suggest that many LDCs are merely pegging to the dollar whereas, in view of their own trade and debt patterns, they should be following more sophisticated pegging tactics, such as a trade-weighted effective exchange rate peg.

Implications of the Oil Price Rise

The massive influence of the oil price rise in late 1973 on the international economy will affect the interests of the developing countries in in-

57. Algeria, Cambodia (Khmer Republic), Malaysia, Morocco, Nigeria, Philippines, Tunisia, Yugoslavia.

58. Brazil, Colombia, Indonesia, Korea, Vietnam.

59. This figure probably overstates the weight of pegging to the dollar in economically meaningful terms. Countries that frequently adjust their rates—such as Brazil, Colombia, and Korea—can take into account trade-weighted exchange rate movements when they set new rates, so that they may be following more sophisticated policies than merely following the dollar even though the dollar is the currency chosen for the peg.

ternational monetary reform. The principal effects are likely to be the following: flexible exchange rates among industrial countries will be all the more important in light of the new need for coping with developments associated with the oil price increase; changes in liquidity resulting in part from the oil price increases make it unlikely that any new SDRs will be created at all and therefore even less likely that aid will be channeled to the LDCs through a link to SDR creation. Furthermore, the heightened need of LDCs for buoyant export demand will make successful international monetary reform all the more significant to them.

The fluidity with which oil exporters can shift their placement of assets and their choice of currency for payment suggests that there will persist a major potential for fluctuations in the relative strengths of currencies in the industrial countries. With rigidly fixed exchange rates such fluctuations could lead to runs on individual currencies and massive shifts in reserves followed by large discrete exchange rate changes. For example, the preference of some Arab nations for assets placement and payment in pounds sterling exerted a buoying influence on that currency during 1974. If this preference were to decline, the resulting downward pressure on the pound would be much more smoothly accommodated with flexible rates than with fixed rates. The latter would provide another easy target for speculators and could result in anticipatory capital outflows from Britain and then a collapse of the newly unrealistic exchange rate.[60]

In short, more flexible exchange rates among industrial countries would appear to have become even more desirable for a smooth functioning of the world economy as a result of the oil price increase. Accordingly, the benefits to be expected by LDCs from the agreements that have been negotiated permitting this flexibility are increased.

Another aspect of the impact of the oil price increases concerns the urgency of export expansion for the LDCs. The price rise inflicts a "transfer" problem on the LDCs that is additional to the "real income loss" problem suffered by the developed countries. Whereas the developed countries can pay for oil in their own currencies or fairly easily borrow from other countries to pay for it, the LDCs have much weaker ratings on creditworthiness and will be under more pressure to pay for the oil out of

60. By November 1975 the pound had sunk to new lows. While changing currency preferences of the oil-exporting countries may have played some role, other factors, particularly rampant inflation in the United Kingdom, have probably been more important in this decline.

increased export earnings rather than out of increased borrowing. Yet this heightened need of LDCs for buoyant demand for their exports occurs precisely at a time when the developed countries will be attempting to protect their own current accounts in order to avoid extremely high trade deficits associated with the higher oil costs.

To THE EXTENT that more flexible rates can smooth adjustment problems, thereby encouraging stable economic expansion in industrial countries and enhancing the prospects for LDC export growth (through both increased demand and the avoidance of import-restricting measures in industrial countries), they should be more strongly endorsed by developing countries in light of the oil price increase.

Conclusion

The empirical evidence indicates no significant welfare loss for the LDCs resulting from the December 1971 and the February 1973 dollar devaluations (since real debt declines equaled or surpassed real reserve losses), and export data suggest that these realignments as well as subsequent floating stimulated or at least did not inhibit LDC exports. Concern among LDCs about increased uncertainty under a flexible-rate system should be tempered with recognition of the fact that such a system may be fundamentally more certain than a fixed-rate system with infrequent but very large exchange rate moves. Indeed, measures of exchange rate fluctuation among industrial nations indicate greater variability during the fixed-rate period 1959:*1*–1973:*1* than during the floating period thereafter. Nor is there a logical basis for the fear that greater rate flexibility would provoke greater real commodity price fluctuations. The concern that flexible rates would carve up the trading world into blocs is unjustified both theoretically (an LDC can adjust its exchange rate by a trade-weighted average of its partners' rate changes) and empirically (the period of floating since 1973 did not witness substantial formation of such blocs). Floating in 1973 led to four main practices: pegging to the dollar, pegging to the SDR (and therefore the dollar before June 1974), and, though substantially less important, flexible LDC rates and pegging to the pound or franc. By mid-1975 by far the dominant practice was pegging to the dollar, and surprisingly few LDCs were pegging to the new SDR composed of a basket of currencies—although it is reasonable to expect that more will do so in the future. Finally, several LDCs with flexible rates are likely to maintain such rates to neutralize their greater-than-average inflation.

LDCs can diversify both their reserve and debt portfolios to reduce exchange rate risks (taking into account the country composition of their trade). LDC traders can utilize forward exchange markets in industrial countries if they wish to hedge against relative movements in major currencies; and LDC governments should be able at little cost to supply forward local currency cover for future export earnings (though not foreign cover for future imports, which themselves need no stimulus or which can be increased by reduced protection if compensation for exchange rate risk is desired).

Most important, orders of magnitude of all possible effects appear to be such that the LDCs have far more to gain from participating in the global benefits of a generally improved world monetary system than they have to lose through specific, indirect injuries caused by the adoption of flexible exchange rates by industrial countries. If ratified by national legislatures, the monetary reform agreements of January 1976 will mean that countries will be free to continue pursuing the flexible exchange rate policies adopted by the industrial nations and by some LDCs in the previous three years, although perhaps with more systematic coordination and intervention to smooth out fluctuations in rates. Whether this experience will prove beneficial or injurious to the LDCs will hinge not on any side effects specific to them but on whether the allowance for flexibility provides a better basis for the international monetary system overall than the alternative system of par values changed infrequently but by large amounts.

CHAPTER THREE

The SDR Aid Link

THOSE CONCERNED with international monetary reform have long been fascinated with the potential for putting to good auxiliary uses the machinery that any mechanism for creating fiat international liquidity would involve. When the Special Drawing Rights mechanism was initially agreed upon in Rio de Janeiro in 1967, that machinery was finally at hand. At that time the idea of linking reserve creation to development assistance did not in general win favor among industrial countries despite sympathy in such notable quarters as the Joint Economic Committee of the U.S. Congress. Policymakers were convinced that development assistance and international liquidity were problems to be handled separately, and that a linkage between the two might destroy confidence in the new form of reserves.

The primary concern was to establish a new asset—internationally agreed upon and controlled—that could overcome what were regarded as the principal drawbacks of the gold exchange standards. First, the asset would avoid reliance on the vagaries of gold mining for the expansion of world liquidity. Second, the gold exchange system possessed an inherent instability, because it required the persistence of deficits in reserve center countries in order to obtain expansion of foreign exchange liquidity, and yet these deficits threw greater and greater doubt on the strength of the reserve currencies.

Although the final agreement on Special Drawing Rights in 1969 contained no explicit link to development assistance, it represented a substantial gain for the developing countries. The rich Group of Ten countries had previously considered the creation of a new reserve asset for distribution only among themselves;[1] therefore, any participation in the Special Drawing Rights system was a victory for the LDCs. Moreover, by basing allocations on IMF quotas the SDR mechanism created de facto a mini-link because shares of the LDCs in IMF quotas substantially exceeded their shares in relevant economic magnitudes.[2] In addition, for the LDCs, the SDR was a better alternative for liquidity expansion than gold re-valuation, because their share of official gold holdings was much smaller than their share of the SDR emissions.

In the deliberations of the Committee of Twenty and in other forums the developing countries insisted that one of their cardinal demands in monetary reform was that SDR creation and development assistance should be linked by shifting to LDCs a part of the share of SDRs formerly going to industrial countries. In mid-1974 the committee issued its final report without reaching final decisions on the link or on most of the other major aspects of monetary reform. Negotiations in the successor Interim Committee, as reviewed above, achieved agreement on revised treatment of gold, a new trust fund for development aid financed by profits on IMF gold sales, and on the legitimacy of floating exchange rates as well as pro-cedures for coordinating intervention to reduce their fluctuations. These decisions again excluded any link between SDRs and aid. That the LDCs nevertheless accepted the agreements appears to have been due in part to a recognition that agreement was necessary in order to obtain the gold sales and trust fund, whereas a link would not generate aid in the medium term because SDRs were unlikely to be created for some time. In future reform negotiations, however, it would be reasonable to expect the devel-oping countries once again to press the demand for a link.

1. See Robert Triffin, "Linking Reserve Creation and Development Assistance," in *Linking Reserve Creation and Development Assistance,* Hearing before the Sub-committee on International Exchange and Payments of the Joint Economic Com-mittee, 91:1 (GPO, 1969), p. 38. Countries in the Group of Ten are Belgium, Canada, France, Germany, Italy, Japan, the Netherlands, Sweden, the United King-dom, and the United States.

2. In 1970, the LDCs held 27.8 percent of IMF quotas, but accounted for only 19.1 percent of total imports and 14.3 percent of total GNP for IMF member countries. (See International Monetary Fund, *International Financial Statistics* [IMF, selected issues], and International Bank for Reconstruction and Development, *World Bank Atlas: Population, Per Capita Product and Growth Rates* [IBRD, 1972].) While export fluctuation is an additional criterion for IMF quotas, unpub-lished statistical examinations show it cannot explain the high LDC share. The only variable capable of doing so is population.

It is improbable that any SDRs will be created for a period of some years because of the international liquidity situation (discussed in chapter 4). In 1975, there were ample or excessive world reserves. This overriding factor means that even if adopted an SDR aid link could provide no development assistance in the near-term future. Nevertheless, fundamental changes in the monetary system must be assessed in light of their impact over very long periods of time. The Bretton Woods system lasted for three decades. Therefore it is important to examine the SDR aid link as a possible component of a new monetary system even though its actual application might begin only after an initial lapse of time.

The purpose of this chapter is to examine the origins and evolution of the idea of a link with particular attention to its most recent incarnation, the LDC proposal to the Committee of Twenty. The arguments for and against the link are evaluated and a model is developed to assess two of them—its effect on payments imbalances and inflation. In a final appraisal, the potentialities of the link as an aid instrument are compared to LDC aid needs; the bargaining strategies of the industrial and developing countries on the issue are considered; and recommendations are made for change in the specific nature of the link proposed by the LDCs in the event that some form of link is adopted in future negotiations.

Evolution of the Link Concept

Other studies have surveyed the evolution of proposals to link creation of international liquidity to the provision of development assistance.[3] The focus here is on one aspect of these prior proposals: their similarities and contrasts to the specific type of link currently advocated by the developing countries.

The mechanism for linking aid to reserve creation favored by the developing countries in the Committee of Twenty discussions had the following features. (1) In the process of SDR creation, an agreed-upon fraction of the SDRs that originally would have gone to developed countries under the IMF quota-based distribution (used for the 1970–72 emissions) would instead be given to developing countries that are IMF

3. See, for example, Y. S. Park, *The Link between Special Drawing Rights and Development Finance,* Essays in International Finance 100 (Princeton University, International Finance Section, 1973); and John Williamson, "Surveys in Applied Economics: International Liquidity," *Economic Journal,* vol. 83 (September 1973), pp. 685–746.

members. (2) These extra SDRs would go directly to the recipient countries; there would be no intermediaries, such as the International Development Association (IDA) or other multilateral aid agencies. (3) The basis for allocation of the extra SDRs among the developing countries would be their individual IMF quotas, with the exception that a relatively larger share would go to a selected list of "least developed countries." (4) The total amount of SDRs created would depend not upon aid needs but solely upon requirements for expansion of international liquidity.[4]

It is illuminating to compare this version of the link with the major historical formulations of the mechanism that provide its intellectual background.

The 1943 Keynes Plan for international monetary reform is frequently cited as the first major reform proposal providing for a link between aid and the international monetary system.[5] In one section of that plan, concerning use of the proposed International Clearing Union for "other international purposes," it was noted that the Union might grant "overdraft facilities" to "international bodies charged with post-war relief, rehabilitation and reconstruction." The overdraft would be financed out of the "Reserve Fund of the Union," supplemented if necessary by "a levy on surplus credit balances . . . [so that] the resources would be provided in the first instance by those countries having credit clearing accounts for which they have no immediate use and are voluntarily leaving idle."[6]

The resources of this reserve fund would appear to have been extremely limited under the Keynes Plan. It would have been fed by a maximum charge of 2 percent on country surplus or deficit balances in the Union. Had it been adopted and were the plan in operation today, such imbalances would therefore have to reach $50 billion to generate the

4. For the LDC position on the SDR aid link see International Monetary Fund, Committee on Reform of the International Monetary System (Committee of Twenty), *International Monetary Reform* (IMF, 1974). This publication, the final report of the Committee of Twenty, explicitly states the position of the LDCs that a link should employ "an increase in their share of SDRs by means of direct country allocations by the International Monetary Fund" (p. 95). The section dealing with the link in the main body of the report ("Outline of Reform") stated that if a link were adopted based on LDC quotas in the IMF, "Link resources so allocated would be distributed to all developing countries in such a way as to be relatively favorable to the least developed countries." (Ibid, p. 17.)

5. *Proposals for an International Clearing Union*, Command Paper 6437 (His Majesty's Stationery Office, 1943).

6. Ibid., IX-39-1, p. 18; cited in John H. Williams, *Postwar Monetary Plans and Other Essays*, "Proposals for an International Clearing Union" (Alfred A. Knopf, 1944), appendix 3, p. 292.

minimum order of magnitude frequently cited for link aid: $1 billion annually. The existence of such imbalances within the Union in turn would have meant failure of the Union to eliminate the accumulation of large surplus or deficit balances within the international monetary system. In short, in view of the very limited aid magnitudes implied, it would be inappropriate to construe the relevant passage in the Keynes Plan as anything other than an extremely modest bow in the direction of a link.

Another important aspect of the Keynes Plan was its reference to additional charges on countries with surplus balances to provide further resources for aid. This arrangement appears to have reflected a realization that a mechanism that deprived deficit countries of reserves they would otherwise enjoy would be detrimental to the monetary system. The current LDC link proposal makes no distinction between advanced countries with deficit and surplus balances; potential reserves would be drawn away from both (in the first instance) to finance the link; and, as shown below, the net impact after respending of link receipts would probably be a modest decline in reserves of deficit countries and a rise in those of surplus countries compared with levels prevailing without such a link.

In 1958 Sir Maxwell Stamp proposed that the International Monetary Fund be empowered to create liquidity by issuing internationally acceptable certificates; these would be given to an aid-coordinating agency (IDA was specifically mentioned in Stamp's 1962 version) that in turn would give them to LDCs, which would use them to purchase goods from the industrial countries. Stamp based his proposal on the premises that underemployment of resources as well as a desire to build up reserves were prevalent in developed countries. The proposal was designed to facilitate this reserve accumulation at minimal real economic cost because the extra output sold to the LDCs would come from otherwise unemployed resources in the industrial countries. In the process much-needed aid funds would be created. In his 1962 revision of the proposal Stamp furthermore proposed that: (1) countries with surplus balances and overfull employment could opt out by informing IDA that LDCs would not be allowed to spend the IMF certificates on their goods; (2) no industrial country would be obligated to accept Fund certificates in excess of its quota (setting a ceiling omitted in the original proposal); and (3) the certificates would be lent to IDA for fifty years, thereby creating an asset (although an illiquid one) backing the increased international liquidity.[7]

---

7. Maxwell Stamp, "The Stamp Plan—1962 Version," *Moorgate and Wall Street* (Autumn 1962), pp. 80–89.

Stamp emphasized that his plan did not hinge on any perceived shortage of international liquidity; rather, it sought to take advantage of underutilized resources, and it accepted the premise that these resources were underemployed because of the conflicting desires among all of the developing countries to achieve balance of trade surpluses simultaneously, which forced deflation upon some of them (those that were "scared to expand . . . domestic demand because of balance of payments considerations"). This concern with underemployment throws into question the relevance of the scheme, especially after the mid-1960s.[8]

In contrast to the Stamp Plan, the current link proposal favored by LDCs would channel SDRs directly, not through IDA; give no special treatment (exemption) to surplus full-employment countries; involve in all likelihood much smaller real magnitudes of aid (Stamp had proposed $3 billion annually, in 1962 prices); and base liquidity creation on world monetary needs (which Stamp considered of secondary importance).

Robert Triffin has been cited as another early advocate of a link, on the basis of his suggestions for monetary reform at the beginning of the sixties.[9] Proposing that a reformed IMF could create liquidity by issuing certificates, Triffin maintained that these funds could be lent as rediscounts or advances to borrowing countries, and also used for open market investments. The latter would initially be concentrated in the United States and the United Kingdom to smooth the transition when dollar and sterling balances formerly held as reserves by third countries were consolidated within the IMF. Eventually, though, a "portion of such investments might even be channeled into relatively long-term investments for economic development through purchases of IBRD bonds or other securities of a similar character."[10] However, bonds of the International Bank for Reconstruction and Development have always been market securities bearing interest rates (comparable to government bonds), and therefore this procedure would have represented only a minimal transfer of real resources from advanced to developing countries (that is, any modest reduction in the interest charges on IBRD loans that might have resulted if

8. However, the United States and other industrial countries passed from an inflationary boom in 1973 to severe recession in early 1975, with unemployment in some countries higher than at any time since the Great Depression. Whether it is therefore timely to dust off the unemployment argument for a link is discussed in detail on pages 72–73.

9. Robert Triffin, *Gold and the Dollar Crisis: The Future of Convertibility* (Yale University Press, 1960).

10. Ibid., pp. 117–18.

the Bank's borrowing costs had been reduced because of an increased demand for the bonds within a market context). Triffin's proposals therefore did not contain an aid link scheme involving the substantial transfer of resources to the LDCs on a grant basis.

In 1966 Scitovsky proposed a link similar to the Stamp Plan but with modifications to improve the economic results.[11] Like Stamp, Scitovsky justified a link in terms of a Pareto optimal marriage of reserve needs of industrial countries plagued by unemployment with development resource needs of the LDCs. Scitovsky's main innovation was his proposal that reserve creation would be limited to purchases of goods from deficit countries with underemployed resources. Operationally, such a deficit country could use its own currency to buy newly created reserves (Fund obligations) from the IMF. This currency would then be turned over to the IDA and granted to developing countries exclusively for the purchase of items from the donor country. By explicitly excluding surplus countries (and even deficit countries without underemployment), Scitovsky built upon Stamp's revision to avoid inflationary results from a link.

Certain features of the Scitovsky proposal are attractive. Most important, the deficit country would acquire reserves through direct purchase with its own currency. This procedure is diametrically opposed to the effect of the current LDC proposal in that Scitovsky's mechanism would directly increase reserve holdings of deficit industrial countries whereas the LDCs' link version would indirectly reduce those holdings (because advanced countries in deficit would forgo some SDRs directly in an initial diversion of newly created SDRs to the link, and then would fail to recover them fully after LDC respending, given their poor trade competitiveness). Other features of Scitovsky's proposal are less appealing: tying the aid reduces its value to recipients (although Scitovsky argues correctly that tied aid is better than none); fungibility of reserves raises the question of whether an LDC's purchases from the donor country are in fact "additional" to those it would otherwise import (an old problem in the aid business); and by implication, the proposal would rule out link resources except when underemployment clearly existed in the deficit countries.

The tacit identification of "deficit" country with "underemployment" in both the Stamp and Scitovsky plans was probably due to the state of the U.S. economy at the time they wrote. A more natural condition of a

---

11. Tibor Scitovsky, "A New Approach to International Liquidity," *American Economic Review*, vol. 56 (December 1966), pp. 1212–20.

deficit country is inflationary overemployment, and indeed the United States was obviously in this situation in the late 1960s.[12]

An important link proposal carrying implicit approval by portions of international officialdom was one developed in 1969 by a group of experts for the United Nations Conference on Trade and Development.[13] The proposal came after an international agreement to create liquidity in the form of SDRs had already been reached, so it had a more realistic base than those suggested in earlier years. The UNCTAD experts refrained from advocating specific link mechanisms, confining themselves to general support of the idea. However, they clearly indicated that SDRs used in a link scheme should be channeled through IDA (in contrast to the direct delivery based on quotas now favored by the LDCs). They noted that contributions based on the SDR receipts of industrial nations could be either in the SDRs themselves or in the currencies of the contributing countries. The report advocated "prior agreement among the governments concerned" on the fraction of SDR receipts to be contributed (implying an involuntary rather than a voluntary link in which each developed country would have the freedom to choose whether to contribute and how much). The UNCTAD group usefully dealt with the conventional argument opposing the link on the grounds that it would be inflationary. Its report noted that the probable amount of aid provided by the link would be on the order of $1 billion a year, so that "the demand for output in the rich countries, which amounted to about $1,700 billion in 1968, would be raised by little more than one half per mille."[14] The inflationary specter thus dismissed, the UNCTAD experts made no proposals to differentiate between industrial countries with surpluses and those with deficits, nor between those with overemployment and those with underemployment. A portion of the SDRs emitted by the IMF would

12. The issue concerns the direction of causation. In a Keynesian system it is true that an exogenous decline in the trade balance feeds directly into multiplied domestic demand shortfall and deflation. However, the relevant causation for the United States in the late 1960s was in the other direction: excess demand provoked a deterioration in the trade balance by boosting imports and making exports less competitive. Given the conversion of authorities to the proposition that foreign balance must not be allowed to dictate domestic unemployment, the latter condition—coexistence of inflation and deficit—is much more likely to be the general case than the former condition (underemployment with a trade deficit).

13. United Nations Conference on Trade and Development, "International Monetary Reform and Co-operation for Development," Report of the Expert Group on International Monetary Issues (United Nations, October 13, 1969; processed).

14. Ibid., p. 25.

be diverted from all developed countries into the link mechanism regardless of circumstances.

At the 1968 IMF annual meetings, Finance Minister Emilio Colombo of Italy noted the critique that the new SDR mechanism excluded a link to development finance and proposed as a solution "a pledge by the main industrial countries to use the part of their reserves corresponding to a portion of their special drawing rights allocations for the replenishment of IDA or for subscription to World Bank bonds."[15] This one-sentence link proposal amounted to a voluntary scheme that would have had the disadvantage of diverting reserves away from industrial countries (in the first instance), whereas the benefits could have been achieved at lower cost by a similar voluntary provision in which each industrial country used its own currency rather than reserves (under the hypothesis, discussed below, that reserves carry a scarcity price above their market quotation in a country's currency).

Fried subsequently advocated a link that would involve agreement among all industrial countries to contribute to IDA amounts in their own currencies based on some proportion of SDRs received in new emissions by the IMF. (Fried suggested 70 percent, to allow coverage of the 30 percent of SDRs that had to be held rather than used under the "reconstitution" rule.)[16]

Finally, another link variant has been premised on the consolidation of the dollar and sterling "overhang" (foreign exchange reserves held by third countries in excess of desired levels) through conversion into SDRs at the IMF. Proposals along these lines involved allocating amounts of SDRs to the LDCs equaling either the amortization of such balances (as Maynard for one suggests)[17] or the annual differential between the interest paid by the IMF on the SDRs resulting from the consolidation and the payments received by the IMF from the United States and United Kingdom as the ongoing interest burden on the consolidated assets.[18]

---

15. "Statement by the Governor of the Fund for Italy," in *Summary Proceedings of the Twenty-third Annual Meeting of the Board of Governors: September 3–October 4, 1968* (IMF, 1968), p. 81.

16. Edward R. Fried, "International Liquidity and Foreign Aid," *Foreign Affairs,* vol. 48 (October 1969), pp. 140–49.

17. See Geoffrey W. Maynard, *Special Drawing Rights and Development Aid,* Overseas Development Council, Occasional Paper 6 (Washington, D.C.: the Council, 1972).

18. This type of link raises the question of whether the United States and the United Kingdom would be prepared to continue paying market interest rates on such

A NUMBER of additional link proposals have been offered by academics and officials, but the variations enumerated above include the principal forms that have been considered.[19] Two salient points emerge in considering the relationship between major past proposals and the current link mechanism favored by developing countries. First, almost all previous proposals provided for the channeling of link aid through IDA or similar agencies. By contrast, the link form favored by the LDCs provides for direct delivery of extra SDRs to the developing countries. This shift insures against outside interference in LDC domestic affairs but offers no guarantee that the funds will be used for efficient development programs. A factor probably contributing to this position is that in the past IDA has tended to distribute the lion's share of its funds to a handful of the poorest countries, expecially India, Indonesia, Pakistan, and Bangladesh. With direct allocation based on LDC quotas in the IMF, a number of much more prosperous developing countries would also receive link funds. They would not have been indifferent to this fact.

Second, by evolving from the "unemployment" basis prominent in early plans to a forthright redistribution mechanism in later versions, the link could be clearly specified as subordinate to the requirements of world liquidity. Thus, while Stamp could state that his plan did not depend on a need for additional world liquidity (and Scitovsky could by implication agree), it is now mandatory to preface any link proposal with a statement confirming that SDR creation must be determined solely by the requirements of international liquidity and not by aid needs.

---

assets if they took on some exchange guarantee in the consolidation; moreover, the rise in the interest rate on the SDR from 1½ percent to 5 percent reduces the scope for a link through this interest differential. Note that the LDCs were reportedly unenthusiastic about consolidation itself during the deliberations of the Committee of Twenty because of an apparent fear that consolidation would generate a surfeit of SDRs and leave no annual emission of SDRs on which a link (of the more common variety) could operate. The lack of enthusiasm may also have been because of a preference for retaining foreign exchange reserves with higher interest yield than the SDR.

19. Those concerned with semantics may wish to note that link proposals have been classified as "organic" if they require a change in the IMF charter permitting direct IMF allocation of SDRs to IDA or the IBRD. Schemes by which advanced countries could instead contribute their own currencies (or their own SDRs) are in contrast "inorganic" but not necessarily "voluntary" (as sometimes named), since a collective agreement to make such contributions could hardly allow for voluntary self-exclusion by individual industrial countries.

Economic Arguments for and against a Link

The central argument for a link between SDR emissions and aid is that it is an instrument for increasing global development assistance. The world total of concessional development aid has stagnated in real terms and declined as a proportion of the gross national product of donor countries. Yet aid needs have been catapulted to higher levels by recent crises in energy and food supply, especially in the newly identifiable fourth world of extreme poverty. The crucial questions are: (1) Would a link actually increase global aid? (2) Could it do so without inflicting indirect costs on the economic system (acknowledging that the direct resource costs corresponding to the aid would have to be borne by donors)?

Aid: Amount, Need, and Quality

Many observers doubt that donor countries would be willing to transfer incremental real resources to the LDCs through an aid link when they would be unwilling to do so through conventional aid channels.[20] One argument that the international monetary mechanism somehow could achieve "incrementality," has been that the link would generate donor willingness to increase aid because it would be executed on a multilateral basis. It might thereby avoid the problems of burden-sharing and terms of trade deterioration considered to be associated with increased bilateral aid.[21] However, this argument supports multilateral aid rather than a link.

Despite protestations to the contrary, there is an abiding theme among advocates of a link that the mechanism could generate, by indirection, aid that otherwise would not be forthcoming from legislative bodies. A comment illustrating this viewpoint is the following:

Chairman Reuss: . . . if you pursue the so-called nonorganic link, I do not see at this moment how you have accomplished very much in political terms that could not be accomplished by a more heroic frontal attack, namely induce the U.S. Congress to pass a law which says we up our miserable present IDA con-

20. See, for example, Harry G. Johnson, "Reserve Creation and Development Assistance," in *Linking Reserve Creation and Development Assistance,* Hearing before the Subcommittee on International Exchange and Payments of the Joint Economic Committee, 91:1 (GPO, 1969), pp. 19–21.

21. See, for example, John Williamson, "Surveys in Applied Economics: International Liquidity," p. 730.

tribution by three times. . . . If, however, we get organic . . . then you may be able to achieve some fiscal monkey business, which would be all to the good.[22]

Here Congressman Reuss not only indicates that it would be desirable to use an aid link to circumvent congressional limitations on directly appropriated aid funds, but he also specifies the means most likely to succeed: an "organic" link with direct flows of SDRs to the multilateral lending agencies rather than an "inorganic" link involving contributions by donor countries of additional conventional aid geared to SDR receipts.

It seems reasonable to assume that the establishment of an SDR aid link would generate some incremental aid but that the incrementality would not be complete. Moreover, the instrument would provide a new excuse for donor countries to hold back on development assistance, using the argument that the international monetary system would now take care of aid. The link mechanism specified by the LDCs—direct emissions of an extra share of SDRs—might be the least likely to reduce other forms of aid, because this process would be separate from the multilateral lending agencies, making it more difficult to argue that the needs of those agencies were being met by the monetary system.

In considering the link in terms of aid needs it is of paramount importance to keep in mind that the magnitude of aid (especially incremental aid) likely to be generated by a link would be very limited. During the first SDR allocation period (1970–72) 3 billion SDRs were issued each year; if half of the three-fourths share allocated to the advanced countries had been diverted to the LDCs, the extra "aid" to the developing countries would have been only 1 billion SDRs. In comparison, the global flow of "official development assistance" (concessional aid) during the period was approximately $8 billion annually. Thus, even without offsetting reductions in other aid, the link would have raised concessional assistance flows by only 12 percent. Advocates of the link within the Committee of Twenty appear to have recognized this limited scope for aid through a link in the following statement of the final report of that body:

It is not envisaged by any of the advocates of an SDR/aid link that resources channeled in this form would provide all, or even necessarily a large part, of the further resource transfer required to support development in the developing countries.[23]

22. Henry S. Reuss in *Linking Reserve Creation and Development Assistance,* Hearing, p. 70.

23. International Monetary Fund, Committee on Reform of the International Monetary System, *International Monetary Reform* (IMF, 1974), p. 96.

Some advocates, however, maintain that even if total aid were not increased whatsoever by the mechanism, it would improve the average quality of aid by virtue of being "untied" (that is, not restricted to purchases in the donor country). This aid quality argument seems now to be more than offset by the mid-1974 decision to raise the interest rate on net use of SDRs from 1½ to 5 percent.[24] Discounted at the conventional 10 percent rate, SDRs would have a grant component[25] of 50 percent. Official development assistance by members of the Organisation for Economic Co-operation and Development has had an average grant element of approximately 80 percent.[26] Therefore, in terms of welfare, $1 of link aid would be worth only 62 cents of conventional aid, an inferiority unlikely to be offset by even high estimates of the higher purchasing power of untied aid.[27]

24. International Monetary Fund, *IMF Survey,* June 17, 1974, p. 185.

25. Ratio of the present discounted value of loan repayments to initial face value of principal.

26. Edwin M. Martin, Organisation for Economic Co-operation and Development, *Development Co-operation: Efforts and Policies of the Members of the Development Assistance Committee,* Report by the chairman of the Development Assistance Committee (Paris: OECD, 1973), p. 54.

27. Of course, it would be possible to provide that interest not be charged on link SDRs (by, for example, reducing the base on which interest payments to net holders of SDRs were calculated and using the savings to pay the interest on net use of link SDRs). (See United Nations Conference on Trade and Development, *Money, Finance and Development: Papers on International Monetary Reform* [United Nations, 1974], pp. 50–52; and Peter Isard and Edwin Truman, "SDRs, Interest and the Aid Link: Further Analysis," *Banca Nazionale del Lavoro Quarterly Review,* no. 108 [March 1974], pp. 88–93.) The major issue involved here is whether the bargaining power of the LDCs (and the desire of the developed countries to provide aid through a link) is sufficiently strong to achieve an agreement providing for the exemption of interest on link SDRs. A minor issue is that the mechanisms creating essentially different categories of SDRs would be awkward although technically feasible. Another issue is whether developed countries would have the appropriate incentive to hold SDRs if their effective average rate of return were reduced by a reduction of the net holding base on which interest were paid to them. (As good marginalist maximizers they would remain unaffected by such a change so long as their holdings were above the threshold where interest receipts began, but they might look at average rather than marginal return when evaluating the desirability of holding SDRs.) Still another consideration is that, based on "the economics of charity," aid is most efficiently given through larger loans at higher interest rates, so long as the rate of return for the recipient exceeds that for the donor. Hence, it would be more efficient to leave the interest rate for link SDRs unaltered (at 5 percent) but to increase the fraction of SDRs allocated to the link. However, to generate the same grant component aid arising from zero interest on link SDRs, it would be necessary to double the proportion of SDRs allocated to a link (compared with a scheme channeling half of former

There are two other important dimensions to aid quality: its effective use and the equity of its allocation. The LDC position favoring direct emission of link SDRs to recipient countries raises the issue of lack of donor influence over the use of the aid. Concern about effective use lay behind the preponderance of schemes providing for link aid channeled through the multilateral lending agencies, in the proposals of academics, officials of some developed countries,[28] and international bodies.[29] The LDCs prefer direct receipt of SDRs because they want no outside interference[30] and because self-interest of the more prosperous LDCs dictates circumvention of the per capita income ceiling on aid through agencies such as IDA.

On the distribution issue, the very nature of the IMF quota system builds in inequitable distribution if link aid is to be allocated on the basis of quotas among LDC recipients. The per capita magnitude of the IMF quotas is closely related to per capita income of member countries, as shown in the scatter diagram, figure 3-1. Economic magnitudes—GNP and trade—form the basis for IMF quotas. The result is that the highest amounts of link aid per capita would go to the richest developing countries included in the scheme (which might even include several "marginal" countries seeking to classify for the scheme, such as Spain and Portugal).

Of the SDRs actually distributed to LDCs on the basis of IMF quotas during the 1970–72 period of emissions, 43 percent went to countries too rich to be eligible for loans from IDA (which then had a cutoff per capita income of $300). Thus, it could be said that the quota-based link desired

---

shares held by industrial countries in SDRs into a link)—which would leave no SDR shares whatsoever for the developed countries. Yet a zero share in SDR allocations would surely bias incentives of advanced nations against the creation of any SDRs whatsoever, despite pledges to do so in accordance with international liquidity needs.

28. For example, the proposal of Emilio Colombo, "Statement by the Governor of the Fund for Italy," in International Monetary Fund, *Summary Proceedings of the Twenty-third Annual Meeting of the Board of Governors, 1968*, p. 81.

29. Such as the recommendation by the group of UNCTAD experts in United Nations Conference on Trade and Development, "International Monetary Reform and Co-operation for Development"; also see Inter-American Committee on the Alliance for Progress (CIAP), *Latin America and the Reform of the International Monetary System* (Washington, D.C.: Organization of American States, 1972).

30. To the LDCs the quality of aid would be higher, rather than lower, if it were automatic and unrelated to any multilateral or bilateral agency's evaluation of recipients' policies.

Figure 3-1. *IMF Quotas per Capita in Relation to Income per Capita for Seventy-two Less Developed Countries*

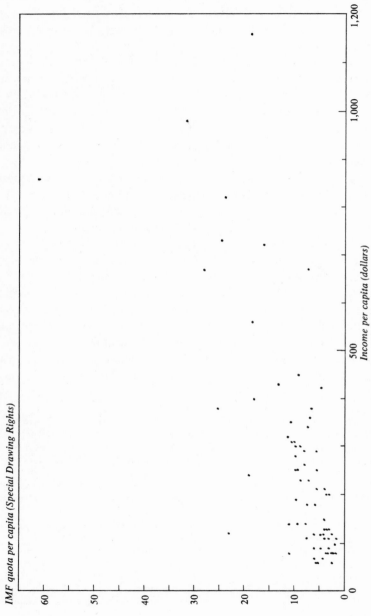

IMF quota per capita (Special Drawing Rights)

Income per capita (dollars)

Sources: International Bank for Reconstruction and Development, *World Bank Atlas: Population, per Capita Product and Growth Rates* (IBRD, 1971) and International Monetary Fund, *International Financial Statistics* (April 1973).

by the LDCs would distribute almost half of the assistance generated through this mechanism to countries insufficiently poor to qualify for the very scarce concessional aid resources of the principal multilateral lending agency.

The LDCs have accepted in principle the proposition that a link would distribute to a selected list of least developed countries a relatively higher share of the aid than the IMF quotas imply. However, as table A-1 indicates, this official list of countries, as defined at the third meeting of UNCTAD, is a token gesture. It excludes countries with populations of over 25 million. It includes countries that altogether received only 6 percent of the SDRs emitted to the LDCs in the 1970–72 period; if their proportional shares of SDRs were increased, it would be at limited cost to the other developing countries.[31]

Finally, if after a link mechanism is introduced, conventional aid declines, and the chief link proposal permits most aid to be channeled to the relatively rich LDCs, there might well be a regressive redistribution of global grant equivalent assistance away from the neediest countries. Such a development would be especially costly in terms of world welfare at a time of increasing relative poverty in the fourth world.

THE SDR AID LINK proposal of the developing countries in the Committee of Twenty would appear to be an inefficient aid instrument. It would not provide for the controls for effective use characteristic of aid through multilateral agencies and other channels. Furthermore, a large portion of the aid would be given to a group of relatively well-to-do countries otherwise ineligible for scarce near-concessional funds. Therefore, in order for this type of link to be attractive from the standpoint of the development assistance objective, one must make the very optimistic assumption that the mechanism would generate incremental aid and would not reduce aid flows that otherwise would materialize in alternative assistance channels. In this optimistic case even this type of link would do some good. In a more pessimistic case, the establishment of the mechanism could do harm to the poorest countries by reducing aid flows through alternative channels that focus on these countries.

31. Although a more meaningful list of "least developed" countries could be drawn up (including, for example, India and Bangladesh), the more prosperous LDCs would probably oppose such a revision since it would deny them the bulk of link aid that they could otherwise expect.

SDRs: Windfall, Seigniorage, and Social Savings

Another basic argument for an SDR link to aid is that, far from being a form of "aid," it would merely be the fair way to distribute gains from the new monetary instrument, the SDR. In its simplest form, the argument maintains that SDRs, like manna from heaven, represent free additional resources to the world economic system and therefore obviously should be given to the poor. This perception gives rise to critiques such as the following: ". . . it is rather conspicuously unfair to give a large share of a valuable free asset to the rich minority, leaving only a small fraction for the large poor majority."[32] But SDRs are not in themselves free goods or additional real resources. They are scrip representing claims on existing resources. They may facilitate the production of extra resources, but they can do so only if their distribution is such that their economic function is fulfilled. They should enable recipients to make balance of payments adjustments without dislocative short-run recessionary measures at the expense of real output growth.

The notion that SDRs are free real resources may be dismissed; none of the serious participants in monetary reform discussions—representatives from either developing or advanced countries—are likely to be sufficiently naive to view them as such.[33] More relevant are the related but more subtle arguments that the creation of SDRs involves (a) seigniorage and (b) social savings, and that these should be distributed to the poor countries. Reviewing the relevant literature, Williamson describes the link in these terms, noting that the substitution of fiat money for commodity money (such as gold) produces a "social saving of the resources that would otherwise have been absorbed in the production of money," and a corresponding gain of seigniorage to the issuer of the fiat money (equal to the excess of what others are willing to pay for the money over the resource cost of producing it). Hence, "the seigniorage resulting from the production of fiduciary reserve assets" represents one of the "few instruments to improve the world distribution of income."[34]

32. James W. Howe, "Let's Spread Them Around," *Foreign Policy*, no. 8 (Fall 1972), p. 102.

33. Note that in the 1974 report of the Committee of Twenty the list of arguments favoring the link contained no passage arguing that SDRs were free resources or a windfall gain that should go to the poor. (In International Monetary Fund, Committee on Reform of the International Monetary System, *International Monetary Reform* [IMF, 1974], pp. 96–97.)

34. John Williamson, "Surveys in Applied Economics," *Economic Journal*, pp. 723, 728.

SEIGNIORAGE. It is important to note that seigniorage appropriately defined involves a simple transfer from one individual or group to others. Creation of fiat money confers on the issuer claims against the real resources of the rest of the community—claims that if exercised transfer real wealth through an inflation tax. The term is thus completely appropriate in describing the SDR and a possible aid link: because the SDR involves seigniorage (that is, a vehicle for creating potential claims), the question is whether that seigniorage will be used to maintain unaltered a preexisting distribution of given resources, as the current IMF quota-based system essentially does, or whether the potential vehicle for redistribution will in fact be used for redistribution.[35] In other words, the creation of SDRs is comparable to an international tax, and the issue is whether to return the tax receipts instantaneously to the individual taxpaying countries or instead to use the new instrument for redistributing tax receipts from the rich countries to the poor.

A variant of the seigniorage argument is the following. Before the existence of the SDR, countries desiring liquidity bought gold or accumulated reserve currencies; the former conferred seigniorage on the gold producers (insofar as their costs fell short of the price of gold), and the latter gave seigniorage gains to the United States and the United Kingdom. An SDR link to aid would merely transfer this seigniorage to the LDCs, so that "non-reserve centers" and "non-producers of gold" would be as well off as before although a net transfer would take place from reserve centers and gold producers to the LDCs. With regard to gold-producing countries this argument appears valid.[36] However, concerning the seigniorage gains of reserve currency countries it appears exaggerated because these gains are questionable in view of the interest burden incurred on outstanding dollar and sterling balances.[37] Correspondingly, the costs to non-reserve

35. Grubel presents a succinct discussion of the analytics of a link, emphasizing that the allocation of SDRs in accordance with countries' long-run demand for reserves—so that on the average each country holds rather than spends its SDRs—is neutral, whereas distribution heavily favoring the LDCs must generate a redistribution of existing wealth toward them. (Herbert G. Grubel, "Basic Methods for Distributing Special Drawing Rights and the Problem of International Aid," *Journal of Finance*, vol. 27 [December 1972], pp. 1009–22.)

36. However, the amount of seigniorage depends on the excess of the monetary value of gold over its mining costs. In mid-1975 marginal gold production costs appear to be well in excess of the "official" price of gold ($42.22) although far below the price in the private market "tier." (See Timothy Green, *The World of Gold Today* [Walker, 1973; rev. ed. of *The World of Gold*].)

37. See, for example, C. Fred Bergsten, *The Dilemmas of the Dollar: The Eco-*

countries of holding such balances (and in the meantime providing goods in return for them) are not necessarily high after considering the interest earned.

SOCIAL SAVINGS. That the issuance of SDRs involves seigniorage therefore does not mean there is a net windfall to the world community available for redistribution to the poor. However, if social savings arise from the creation of SDRs, such a net windfall does exist. From the standpoint of the world as a whole, formation of a monetary system that forgoes the need to mine gold permits a social saving of resources. The resources thereby saved might be transferred to the developing countries. However, no supporters of the link appear to be confining the recommended link aid to that portion of the liquidity created that would represent resources saved by ceasing to mine gold.

Johnson has argued that the social savings of SDRs relative to gold mining are in any case irrelevant in evaluating link proposals, because the appropriate alternative is the creation of SDRs with a neutral distribution that involves no resource costs and no resource transfers.[38] This position begs the question of the legitimacy from a welfare standpoint of creating the original SDR system in the first place. That system distributed the social savings relative to gold across countries approximately in proportion to the preexisting world income distribution, not according to need. However, the fact remains that the SDR now exists as an alternative to gold, and it very well might not have been agreed upon in the first place had a wealth redistributional feature been imposed.

A more pragmatic consideration on social savings relative to gold is that, at the present time, world liquidity could easily be increased merely by setting a new official price of gold at the free market price. This price far exceeds the old official price of \$42.22 an ounce, which is to be abolished in any event.[39] This "creation of official liquidity" through gold revaluation in the first instance would involve no dedication of additional real resources to mining since the relevant price determining the incentive to produce gold already exceeds (or equals) that to which a new official

nomics and Politics of United States International Monetary Policy* (New York University Press for the Council on Foreign Relations, 1976), chap. 7.

38. Harry G. Johnson, "The Link that Chains," *Foreign Policy*, no. 8 (Fall 1972), pp. 113–20.

39. The agreements of the Interim Committee in August 1975 and January 1976

price would be moved.[40] That such a decision would involve unfortunate distributional consequences (in part because the LDCs have a very small share of gold reserves) does not alter the fact that it would constitute liquidity creation at no real resource cost.

Finally, the argument that the SDR avoids the loss of resources in gold mining has lost relevance for an additional reason: foreign exchange has very probably become a more viable alternative reserve form as the result of the end of the Bretton Woods system, and the creation of reserves in the form of foreign exchange requires no wasting of real resources. Under the system of fixed exchange rates and gold convertibility, foreign exchange reserves were inherently unreliable because their very accumulation put mounting balance of payments pressure on the reserve center currency and threatened sudden collapse of the value of that currency. Under flexible rates without gold convertibility there is no such potential for collapse through a run on the reserve center's currency. In fact, there is now a new reason for holding foreign exchange reserves. The SDR now equals a basket of specified currencies, and it seems likely that countries will soon realize that they can do better than the SDR by holding as reserves a similarly proportioned basket of assets denominated in the same currencies as the SDR. This conglomerate foreign exchange reserve asset would pay a higher interest rate than the SDR (at the present and under likely future conditions in monetary markets) and, at the same time, provide the same degree of security.

There is another sense in which the SDR may be said to generate a social saving: by increasing reserves, the SDR may smooth adjustment to balance of payments problems and permit the avoidance of real output reductions. This "real output effect" depends, as mentioned above, on which countries receive the extra reserves. To minimize loss of real output

---

provide for the abolition of the official price of gold and, if ratified, would permit central banks to make gold transactions at prices other than the official price. See page 99 for further details on the agreements concerning gold.

40. To the extent that private expectations of a still higher price would be reinforced by an increase in the official price, there could be some increase in real resources dedicated to gold mining; but such activity in response to a given percentage increase in the official price would almost certainly be much lower under current circumstances than that which would occur if the market and official prices were equal.

this additional liquidity should be distributed in proportion to long-run reserve demand (without going to the extreme of rewarding poor policies by distributing SDRs only to those countries experiencing deficits). To the extent that agreement by all parties is necessary to create SDRs, it may be said that LDC participation enables some advanced countries to reduce the recessionary output losses they otherwise would experience, and that part of this social gain should be paid to the LDCs in return for their co-operation.[41] Of course, by receiving SDRs the LDCs already enjoy such benefits with regard to their own economies; the issue that the creation of a link mechanism raises is whether LDCs should in addition receive a portion of the same type of recession-avoidance gains accruing to the ad-vanced countries. This situation amounts to a game-theoretic setting in which the LDCs can inflict on the advanced nations an injury equal to the output that would be forgone in industrial countries if SDRs were not created, and therefore the LDCs may be able to extract from the de-veloped countries a side payment of an amount less than or equal to the extent of this injury.

To place the "output effect" of extra liquidity into perspective, it is useful to consider likely magnitudes. Of a given addition to world liquidity, a portion will go to reserves in countries with surplus balances and another portion to those with deficit balances, either as direct allocations or indirectly through induced export earnings. Since the LDCs tend to respend extra foreign exchange, the bulk of these final reserve effects will be in the industrial countries. Suppose that on the average the developed countries with surplus balances receive one-half of the extra liquidity and those with deficit balances the other half.[42] Then half of the extra liquidity has no "output effect" because the surplus countries are under no pressure

41. Thus, the UNCTAD group of experts argued: "To the extent that interna-tional action can result, over time, in the creation of additional resources, and the fuller utilization of existing resources, it seems equitable that at least part of the re-sulting additional output should be channeled to the developing countries." (United Nations Conference on Trade and Development, *International Monetary Reform and Co-operation for Development,* p. 19.)

42. The assumption follows from the fact that the aggregate surplus of the former must equal the aggregate deficit of the latter, abstracting from net surpluses of the developed countries vis-à-vis the LDCs (as is appropriate if the aggregate aid effort and capital flow to LDCs are approximately equally divided between developed countries with surplus and deficit balances). Empirically this division is verified in the simulations discussed below, which find that approximately half of extra SDRs would go directly or indirectly to a group identified as deficit developed countries, with or without a link; the other half would accrue to countries in surplus or inter-mediate positions. See tables 3-2 and 3-5.

to curtail real output to salvage their balance of payments position. As for the other half, the output effect depends on the "shadow price of foreign exchange" in the deficit countries—the real increase in their gross national products made possible by the availability of an extra unit of foreign exchange.[43] Estimating the excess of this scarcity price over the market exchange rate is extremely difficult, but it is unlikely that the scarcity premium will be greater than, say, 25 percent or at the most 50 percent.[44] If an upper bound of the output effect of extra liquidity to deficit countries were set at 50 percent of the face value, then with a given emission of SDRs, 50 percent of one-half would amount to the real output gains for the world economy. The remaining three-quarters of the face value of the extra SDRs would merely be a vehicle for shuffling claims among countries against existing resources. If a link were to be advocated on grounds that poor countries should receive the extra world output resulting from greater liquidity, then using the above example a link should be confined to only 25 percent of the extra SDRs created. These figures are merely illustrative, but they indicate the type of analytical work required before a net output gain from SDRs can be identified and, thus, before this gain can be used as the basis for determining what portion of new SDRs to divert to an aid link.

THOSE WHO argue that SDRs contribute a windfall benefit to the world that should be given to the poor countries are on shaky ground. In the first instance SDRs are merely scrip permitting claims on existing resources (through the power of seigniorage). The social savings afforded by abstaining from gold production in meeting new liquidity needs are of little relevance now that extra liquidity based on existing gold could be achieved by reestablishing an official price close to the market price. Also, the creation of reserves through the accumulation of foreign exchange (which

---

43. Although the concept of a shadow price of foreign exchange is common in the literature dealing with developing countries, it is rarely applied to the economics of industrial countries. In the situation described here, however, the concept is applicable. For example, if the exchange rate is 5 francs to the dollar, but the acquisition of 5 francs permits relaxation of restrictive measures and an increase of 25 cents in domestic economic activity in the United States, then the "shadow price" for the franc would be 4 francs to the dollar (25 percent above the market rate).

44. A clue to the scarcity premium may be found in the subsidy factor in national programs designed to earn foreign exchange, such as export credit subsidies and tax programs like the Domestic International Sales Corporation scheme in the United States.

involves no real resource cost globally) now appears to be a more viable alternative than under the Bretton Woods system. The world output gains to be derived from extra liquidity might provide the basis for determining what portion of SDR emissions to allocate to a link. However, these output gains will constitute only a fraction of the face value of the increased liquidity. This fraction will depend on the portion of SDRs accruing directly and indirectly to the countries with deficit balances, and on the scarcity premium for the real value of foreign exchange in those countries.

Unemployment and Competitive Surpluses

Another argument that has been made for the link is the proposition that most industrial countries seek current account surpluses that in the aggregate exceed the amount of aid and capital flows they are prepared to direct toward the LDCs. As a result, according to the argument, the industrial countries' surplus targets are incompatible, and some of these countries must experience lower surpluses and therefore lower aggregate demand than they desire.[45] The consequence will be an increase in deflationary pressure. Scitovsky and many others have based their advocacy of a link on this underemployment argument.[46]

At least before late 1974, it was difficult to give weight to the underemployment arguments in the face of inflationary excesses in the world economy. Various authors pointed out that the argument was outdated.[47] To be sure, the Bretton Woods system has long been considered to have had a deflationary bias because of the unequal status of deficit countries

45. For a statement of this argument on incompatible surplus targets see Sidney Dell, "The Case for the 'Link'," in *Linking Reserve Creation and Development Assistance,* Hearing, pp. 19–21.

46. Maxwell Stamp, "The Stamp Plan—1962 Version," pp. 80–89; and Tibor Scitovsky, "A New Approach to International Liquidity," pp. 1212–20.

47. See, for example, Harry G. Johnson, "The Link That Chains," p. 116. Rejection of the "underemployment" argument is not inconsistent with identification of a real output effect of providing extra liquidity to deficit countries that as a result can forgo curtailment of output. The difference is that the former argument asserts that a shortfall from the target trade surplus will exert a downward Keynesian multiplier deflationary effect: hardly a problem in recent years, given the abundance of other inflationary demand elements. The latter proposition in contrast considers aggregate demand adequate or excessive as a longer-run matter, but recognizes the fact that attempts to compress payments adjustment into very short periods for lack of reserves may prohibit achievement of full capacity utilization.

under pressure to deflate their economies and surplus countries with no corresponding pressure to reduce their surpluses by inflating their own.[48] More recently, the system has been viewed as inherently inflationary, because the unwillingness of modern governments to accept deflation has meant that equilibrium under fixed exchange rates could be achieved only by inflation in surplus countries.[49] From this perspective, the move to flexible rates offers the opportunity to avoid an inflationary bias, although quite the contrary bias is seen by others, who maintain that flexible rates remove the balance of payments discipline present under fixed rates that acted as a restraint on inflationary pressures.

Given the development of severe recession in the United States and other industrial countries in 1975, the unemployment argument for the linking of SDRs to aid might appear to merit reexamination. The argument might even be made that creating a link would be a painless contribution to recovery, because unlike most stimulative measures it would involve no increase in the federal deficit and therefore would not further burden the money markets, raise interest rates, nor present the monetary authorities with the unpleasant choice of either dampening recovery by allowing interest rates to rise or else inviting future bursts of inflation by an accommodating expansion of the money supply.

Nevertheless, the proposition that a link should be established to fight unemployment lacks force even within the recent context of recession. Inconsistent attempts by developed countries to reach trade surpluses did not cause the recent recession.[50] Therefore, the traditional argument for the link as a means of allowing the developed countries to achieve trade surpluses is irrelevant. More fundamentally, unemployment is a temporary phenomenon, for which major alternative remedies exist (such as the 1975 tax cut in the United States). Given the time lag required to establish new international mechanisms, the 1974–75 recession would

48. For example, the Keynes Plan, see *Proposals for an International Clearing Union*.

49. Gottfried Haberler, "Two Essays on the Future of the International Monetary Order," p. 9.

50. Instead, in the United States the recession owed much to the rise in oil prices, which acted as an enormous excise tax sopping up potential consumer demand while at the same time crippling automobile sales. In addition, tight money policy boosted interest rates and depressed the housing sector. Furthermore, the prior inflationary phase appears to have induced the buildup of exaggerated inventories (a classic hedge during inflation), leading to a typical inventory cycle downturn once inflationary expectations declined.

most probably be well past by the time any link funds would be available (let alone spent); and the probable result would be (as in the case of so many other anticyclical remedies) that such funds would add demand to a new boom phase already replacing the recessionary trough.

THE NOTION that a permanent instrument such as an SDR aid link can be justified in terms of fighting unemployment must either presume that unemployment is permanent or that the link would itself be sporadic and limited to very infrequent medicinal doses during the rare spells of recessionary infirmity of the international economy. The former is unlikely, and in the latter case the link would be too limited and unpredictable an instrument to contribute significantly to aid needs.

Other Arguments Favoring a Link

In addition to the major arguments examined above favoring a link of SDR emissions to aid, two others warrant consideration. The first concerns the relationship of a donor's aid effort to its balance of payments constraint; the second deals with technical aspects of IMF quotas and the demand for reserves.

BALANCE OF PAYMENTS CONSTRAINT ON AID. Dell and Maynard among others have maintained that industrial countries would like to have given more aid in recent years but did not do so because of possible repercussions on their balance of payments.[51] The link is thus proposed as a means of giving aid without subjecting a donor country to potential reserve loss. However, the logic of this argument depends upon the system against which it is being compared; for if the alternative is SDRs without a link the net impact on a donor's reserves of aid through the link may be negative.[52]

Therefore donors truly concerned about balance of payments are likely to prefer SDRs to which no link is attached, combined with their own contributions of tied bilateral aid or multilateral aid through institutions in which their share of procurement (LDC purchases of goods and services using aid funds) exceeds their share in contributions.

51. Sidney Dell, "The Case for the 'Link'," in *Linking Reserve Creation and Development Assistance,* Hearing, p. 6; and Geoffrey W. Maynard, *Special Drawing Rights and Development Aid.*
52. As pointed out by Henry S. Reuss in *Linking Reserve Creation and Development Assistance,* Hearing, p. 63.

EXPORT FLUCTUATIONS. Cohen has argued for a link on the grounds that developing countries should receive a higher share in the SDRs than at present because their export fluctuations are greater than those of developed countries, and because other aspects of their economies also impose greater relative difficulty of adjustment so that their long-run demand for reserves is relatively higher than that of industrial countries.[53] However, this argument implies not a link but an examination of the weight attached to export instability and other specific elements in the assignment of IMF quotas. Moreover, as noted above, the LDCs already enjoy larger shares in IMF quotas and SDRs than either their share of GNP or trade among IMF members would warrant, and it seems doubtful that fine-tuning to account for greater export fluctuation and the like would boost their SDR shares still further. Furthermore, the argument essentially refers to reserves for "holding," not reserves for spending, so that its relevance to the link is limited; SDRs linked to aid are intended to transfer actual resources to the LDCs.

Effect on Confidence in SDRs and the Amount Created

Early and persistent objections to the link have been that it would undermine confidence in the SDR as well as distort decisions on the appropriate amount to be created.[54] After more than five years of experience with the SDR system and the net use of SDRs by developing countries within that system, the "confidence" objection to the link appears quite weak,[55] as noted in the report of the Committee of Twenty.[56] Also, there has been unanimous acceptance among participants in monetary reform discussions that the amount of SDRs created would be determined solely

53. Benjamin J. Cohen, *Adjustment Costs and the Distribution of New Reserves,* Princeton Studies in International Finance 18 (Princeton University, International Finance Section, 1966).

54. See the Group of Ten's "Ossola Report," especially paragraphs 120 and 138. (Group of Ten, *Report of the Study Group on the Creation of Reserve Assets,* Rinaldo Ossola, chairman [Rome: Bank of Italy, May 1965].)

55. Some would argue that with each passing year in which no SDRs are created (the last emission of SDRs was in 1972), the "confidence" in the asset declines. However, recent changes in the asset—denomination by a basket of currencies and an increase in its interest rate—should have improved its relative attractiveness and strengthened confidence in the SDR.

56. International Monetary Fund, Committee on Reform of the International Monetary System, *International Monetary Reform* (IMF, 1974), p. 99.

on the basis of world liquidity needs (with development requirements absorbing any resulting fluctuations in the availability of funds), and the requirement for an 85 percent majority in voting on SDR allocations should ensure that excess emissions do not result from pressures for development finance. Indeed, the more likely problem regarding SDR creation is that the developed countries would see less direct benefit for themselves in SDR emissions that must pass through a link, and accordingly would approve the creation of a smaller amount of SDRs with a link mechanism than without it.

Inflation

Another argument against the link, which has been instrumental in official opposition to its adoption, has been the fear that by generating extra world demand the mechanism would be inflationary. This concern has been Germany's major objection to the link;[57] the United States has also voiced this argument on various occasions. The objection is particularly surprising in view of the great frequency with which economists have pointed out that even the largest conceivable link allocations would be trivial relative to world GNP.[58] This persistent apprehension may be attributable to the belief that even though incremental demand would appear minuscule when compared to global aggregates, it could generate inflationary pressures for a handful of countries, such as Germany and Japan, if LDC purchases were concentrated on the exports of these countries. This concern is examined empirically in the model described on pages 77 to 87 through simulations of the effects of alternative link schemes on exports and reserves of individual advanced countries. This study finds that the inflation fear remains wholly unwarranted because even for countries with greatest relative concentration of link respending, the resulting increment in export demand is inconsequential relative to the existing export levels.

Another possible basis for the lingering fear of inflation involves the

---

57. Helmut Schmidt, "Statement by the Governor of the Bank for Germany," in International Monetary Fund, *Summary Proceedings of the Twenty-eighth Annual Meeting of the Board of Governors, September 1973* (IMF, 1973), p. 52.

58. For example, UNCTAD, "International Monetary Reform and Co-operation for Development," pp. 23–26; Sidney Dell, in *Linking Reserve Creation and Development Assistance,* Hearing, pp. 5–12; Robert Triffin, in ibid., pp. 37–42; and Geoffrey W. Maynard, *Special Drawing Rights and Development Aid.*

whole system of SDRs. There was substantial European opposition to the establishment of SDRs in the first place, on the grounds that the new mechanism would merely allow the United States and the United Kingdom to continue in their profligate ways by easing the financing of their payments deficits. However, countries desiring to limit the availability of SDRs to the United States, the United Kingdom, or other industrial countries, ought to support rather than oppose the link since it reduces availability of SDRs to these countries, at least on the initial round of SDR emission.

Aggravation of Payments Imbalances

A final argument against the link, which has received relatively little attention,[59] is that it is more likely to aggravate than ameliorate the problem of balance of payments adjustment among industrial countries. SDRs received as link aid are more likely to be respent by developing countries in industrial countries having surpluses than in those suffering deficits, because the former will tend to be more competitive in the supply of goods. Although the regime of managed floating of exchange rates that began in 1973 should reduce this negative effect by reducing the degree of payments imbalances in the first place, the present system by no means eliminates problems of adjustment. The well-known difficulty of time lags (the J curve) in which devaluation may lead initially to deterioration rather than improvement in payments balance complicates the process of adjustment even with flexible rates. Furthermore, intervention by monetary authorities means that some of the disequilibrium characteristics of the fixed-rate regime remain even under current conditions. Therefore, if a link would seriously aggravate initial payments imbalances, it would represent an unwelcome encumbrance to an already unsteady monetary system.

Concentration of link aid respending in surplus countries has received some attention by economists but usually from a different vantage point. Scitovksy and Triffin implied that such respending would be highly concentrated on exports from the surplus countries; if this were so, it would indeed seriously aggravate the adjustment problem.[60] However, it is much

59. However, this point has been recognized in the deliberations of the Committee of Twenty. (See International Monetary Fund, Committee on Reform of the International Monetary System, *International Monetary Reform*, p. 99.)

60. Tibor Scitovsky, "Linking Reserve Creation and Development Assistance," in *Linking Reserve Creation and Development Assistance*, Hearing, p. 33; and Robert

more reasonable to expect that link respending would follow the general pattern of recipients' marginal trade shares, and although these might be lower than average trade shares for deficit country suppliers, there would still be no binary division in which all respending went to surplus and none went to deficit countries. This assessment is borne out in the empirical simulations discussed on pages 77 to 87.

Scitovsky's concern stemmed from two considerations: first, the optimal way to create world liquidity would be through respending SDRs in countries with unemployment,[61] because the resulting resource transfers would be costless; and second, the threat of respending in surplus countries afraid of inflation would make the latter oppose adequate creation of SDRs.[62] In practice, however, Scitovsky's approach would have meant no creation of SDRs at all: he recommended that they be created only for spending in those developed countries that had both unemployment and payments deficits. In recent inflationary times when the deficit countries were experiencing overfull employment no major industrial country would have qualified under these criteria as an appropriate place for the spending of new SDRs received by LDCs.[63] Finally, exclusive attention to the inflationary impact of respending in surplus developed countries misses the broader problem posed by such a respending pattern. The widening gap of payments imbalances aggravates adjustment difficulties for the deficit countries as well. They lose reserves that would accrue to them under a more neutral SDR allocation system.

THE "PAYMENTS IMBALANCE aggravation" effect of a link is like the inflation impact: it should be valid in direction, but its importance for policy

Triffin in ibid., p. 76. Scitovsky justified the prognosis on grounds that link funds passing through IDA had to be spent on purchases from the lowest bidder, which would necessarily be an exporter from a surplus country. That this is an oversimplification is evident in empirical studies showing that IDA procurement (and similar procurement in other lending agencies) closely parallels average trade patterns insofar as supplier country shares are concerned (see U.S. National Advisory Council on International Monetary and Financial Policies, *Annual Report to the President and the Congress, July 1, 1972–June 30, 1973* [GPO, 1973], p. 24).

61. Scitovsky, "A New Approach to International Liquidity."

62. Scitovsky in *Linking Reserve Creation*, pp. 33, 66.

63. Haberler has made the same point, concluding that a link according to Scitovsky would therefore produce little aid. (Gottfried Haberler, "The Case against the Link," *Banca Nazionale del Lavoro Quarterly Review*, no. 96 [March 1971], p. 18.) Note that the assessment here abstracts from the recent recessionary period of late 1974 and the first half of 1975.

decision depends on its likely empirical magnitude. The following section examines this magnitude, as well as that of the inflation effect.

A Model of the Link's Effect on Payments Imbalances and Inflation

SDRs channeled through a link to aid would tend to be respent by recipient LDCs in advanced countries already enjoying current account surpluses (since their goods would be more competitive than those of deficit countries), raising excess reserves of the surplus countries and reducing still further the reserve positions of the deficit countries (in comparison to the situation under SDR distributions based on IMF quotas). Another disadvantage that has been cited for the link is that it could be inflationary for industrial countries. Unlike several of the other considerations on the merits of the link, these two effects can be examined empirically. To evaluate the magnitudes it is useful to reconstruct the pattern of reserve changes that would have occurred during the 1970–72 period of emission of SDRs if a link had then been in force.

Nature of the Model

For a given amount of global SDR emissions, the change in reserves of an industrial country will be composed of two parts: first, its direct allocation of SDRs from the IMF and, secondly, an indirect component of SDRs "earned" when the LDCs purchase its goods with their receipts of new SDRs. This formulation assumes that the developed countries hold their new SDRs as reserves, whereas the LDCs spend their SDRs on imported goods vital to their economies (although a small allowance must be made for "leakage" of SDRs into LDC reserves).

In view of this formulation of direct and indirect effects of an SDR emission on the reserves and exports of industrial countries, it is possible to calculate the net effect that the establishment of an SDR aid link would have on the exports and reserves of advanced countries. The model used for this purpose is described in appendix B. The effects on reserves and exports are examined using alternative distribution profiles for SDRs: one conforming to the past allocation of SDRs, and two alternatives corresponding to variations of the SDR aid link mechanism. The differences between reserve and export patterns under the original allocation, on the one hand, and under a link, on the other, identifies the net impact of a link. The calculations are for the purpose of testing two hypotheses: (1) that a link would aggravate the imbalance of reserves between deficit and surplus industrial countries; and (2) that additional exports from industrial countries commanded by purchases with SDRs linked to aid would exert inflationary pressures on developed nations.

In both the two alternative SDR distribution profiles under a link, the share of SDRs going to advanced countries (originally 74.8 percent) is cut in half, and the aggregate SDRs of the developing countries increased accordingly (leaving a revised distribution of 37.4 percent of the SDRs to advanced and 62.6 percent to developing countries). In the first link considered (link A), the distribution of SDRs among less developed countries is proportional to their original shares in SDR allocations (and hence to their IMF quotas). This pattern is the one proposed by the LDCs themselves, except that their formal proposal provides for a higher participation of a defined list of least developed countries. Upon examination of the countries thus defined (at UNCTAD III in Resolution 62), it is clear that the magnitudes involved are quite minor (see table A-1). The least developed accounted for only 6 percent of the SDRs allocated to developing countries in the first allocation period; therefore, even a doubling of the relative share among LDCs for the least developed would leave the country distribution profile almost unaltered. This first link variant —the LDC quota variant—is thus representative of the version preferred by the developing countries themselves. A second link variant examined (link B) uses country shares in total concessional lending from multilateral lending institutions during the period 1969–71. In this variant, a developing country's SDR share is in two parts: its original share in SDR allocations and its "multilateral concessional lending" share applied to the extra SDRs channeled to LDCs through the link. Lending data for the International Development Association, the Fund for Special Operations (FSO) of the Inter-American Development Bank, and the Special Fund (SF) of the Asian Development Bank are used for this purpose. This link variant is consistent with the most common proposals by representatives of the developed countries and academics in discussions of the link proposal before that based on quotas was submitted by the developing countries to the Committee of Twenty.

Table 3-1 presents data for the countries examined of the SDR shares under the original allocation (1970–72) and under the two alternative link schemes described above. Other data pertaining to the calculations (ratios of reserves to imports, and marginal trade shares) are given in tables A-2 and A-3, respectively.

Effect of a Link on Reserves Imbalances: Results

The results of the simulation exercise are presented in tables 3-2, 3-3, and 3-4. They are based on a hypothetical SDR emission of 1 billion SDRs, with the effects shown in millions of SDRs. Table 3-2 reports the impact of such an emission on the reserves of developed countries, under the six cases examined. Three alternative SDR allocations are used: the original distribution formula, link *A,* and link *B.* For each of these distributions, the import spending patterns of LDCs are calculated under two alternatives: first, a marginal pattern, representing incremental supplier allocation per unit of incremental imports, and, second, an average pattern representing average import propensities by supplier. The marginal pattern is preferable theoretically but subject to more estimation error, so that the average pattern is included as a check on the results.

The reserve impact, shown in table 3-2, includes two components: direct SDR receipts and indirect receipts earned from exports to the LDCs. This division is clear when table 3-2 is compared with table 3-3, which shows the impact of the 1 billion SDR emission on the exports of the developed countries under the three variants considered. Under the link alternatives, developed countries' exports generated are much larger than under the original pattern of SDR allocation (because more SDRs are being "earned" rather than directly received). Finally, table 3-4 shows the impact of the SDR emission on reserves and imports for the LDCs examined.

In order to examine the hypothesis that the link could aggravate payments imbalances, the results concerning the impact on reserves are aggregated into three classes of advanced countries: those with balance of payments fundamentally in surplus positions, those in equilibrium or "intermediate" positions, and those in fundamentally deficit positions. The basis for these groupings is the exchange rate behavior of each country in the December 1971 Smithsonian realignment. Those countries that remained with the dollar are classified as having been under payments deficit pressures; those that appreciated relative to the dollar by approximately the amount of the appreciation of gold are classified as intermediate cases; and those that appreciated by a substantially larger proportion are grouped as countries under surplus pressures. The United Kingdom is an exception;

Table 3-1. *Percentage Shares by Country of Special Drawing Rights Allocated under Actual and Two Alternative Distributions, 1970–72*[a]

Country	Actual	Link A[b]	Link B[c]
Developed countries			
United States	24.70	12.35	12.35
United Kingdom	10.83	5.42	5.42
Canada	3.86	1.93	1.93
Japan	4.06	2.03	2.03
Industrial Europe			
Austria	0.83	0.41	0.41
Belgium	2.25	1.13	1.13
Denmark	0.89	0.45	0.45
France	5.22	2.61	2.61
Germany	5.84	2.92	2.92
Italy	3.42	1.71	1.71
Netherlands	2.55	1.27	1.27
Norway	0.82	0.41	0.41
Sweden	1.15	0.58	0.58
Other developed areas			
Finland	0.66	0.33	0.33
Greece	0.50	0.25	0.25
Ireland	0.42	0.21	0.21
Spain	1.36	0.68	0.68
Turkey	0.54	0.27	0.27
Yugoslavia	0.75	0.37	0.37
Australia	2.43	1.21	1.21
New Zealand	0.75	0.37	0.37
South Africa	0.96	0.48	0.48
Developing countries			
Latin America			
Argentina	1.80	4.47	2.51
Bolivia	0.15	0.38	0.86
Brazil	1.80	4.47	4.83
Chile	0.65	1.60	0.87
Colombia	0.64	1.59	1.95
Costa Rica	0.13	0.32	0.54
Dominican Republic	0.17	0.42	0.84
Ecuador	0.13	0.33	1.44
El Salvador	0.14	0.34	1.00
Guatemala	0.14	0.35	0.14
Jamaica	0.21	0.52	0.51
Mexico	1.47	3.64	3.82
Panama	0.15	0.36	0.71
Peru	0.48	1.19	1.79
Trinidad and Tobago	0.25	0.61	0.62
Uruguay	0.28	0.70	0.47

Table 3-1 (*continued*)

Country	Actual	Link A[b]	Link B[c]
	Developing countries (continued)		
Venezuela	1.33	3.29	2.82
Middle East			
Egypt	0.77	1.91	1.18
Iran	0.73	1.81	0.73
Iraq	0.27	0.68	0.27
Israel	0.51	1.25	0.51
Syria	0.20	0.50	0.20
Asia			
Afghanistan	0.15	0.38	0.49
Burma	0.25	0.61	0.25
Cambodia (Khmer Republic)	0.12	0.31	0.42
India	3.85	9.56	13.68
Indonesia	1.06	2.64	5.40
Korea	0.26	0.65	0.90
Malaysia	0.72	1.78	0.75
Pakistan and Bangladesh	0.96	2.39	3.69
Philippines	0.61	1.51	0.65
Sri Lanka	0.40	1.00	0.92
Thailand	0.34	0.84	0.34
Vietnam, Republic of	0.23	0.58	0.31
Africa			
Algeria	0.48	1.18	0.48
Ghana	0.36	0.88	0.69
Ivory Coast	0.17	0.42	0.17
Kenya	0.18	0.46	0.52
Morocco	0.46	1.15	0.57
Nigeria	0.54	1.34	0.54
Senegal	0.13	0.33	0.36
Sudan	0.29	0.73	0.29
Tanzania, United Republic of	0.17	0.42	0.69
Tunisia	0.17	0.43	0.55
Uganda	0.16	0.41	0.58
Zaire	0.46	1.15	0.46
Zambia	0.29	0.72	0.29
Total	100.0	100.0	100.0

Sources: First column, calculated from International Monetary Fund, *International Financial Statistics*, August 1973; second and third columns, see text for explanation.

a. Shares reported here are those used for text calculations. They include an expansion factor to account for countries participating in SDR scheme but not directly included in the analysis. (The expansion factor is 1.0029 for developed countries, 1.0993 for developing countries.)

b. The distribution of SDRs to the developing countries under the link mechanism is proportional to their original shares in SDR allocations (related to their IMF quotas).

c. The distribution of SDRs to the developing countries under the link mechanism is based on LDC shares of total concessional lending from multilateral institutions, 1969–71.

Table 3-2. *Effect of an Emission of One Billion SDRs on the Reserves of Selected Industrial Countries under 1970-72 and Two Alternative Distributions*

Millions of SDRs

Country	Increase in reserves using marginal trade shares			Increase in reserves using average trade shares		
	Original	Link A[a]	Link B[b]	Original	Link A[a]	Link B[b]
United States	325.0	317.3	344.4	333.0	337.1	360.1
United Kingdom	131.1	110.7	107.5	137.7	127.2	121.0
Canada	47.6	41.7	38.8	47.0	40.2	42.9
Japan	78.9	115.3	124.9	70.6	94.8	99.8
Industrial Europe						
Austria	9.8	7.9	7.4	9.9	8.3	6.9
Belgium	28.4	25.7	24.0	28.2	25.4	22.6
Denmark	10.8	9.3	8.6	10.6	8.6	8.3
France	68.6	66.7	61.0	68.5	66.5	55.9
Germany	91.1	110.4	103.8	88.4	103.6	102.5
Italy	42.7	38.1	33.8	46.0	46.3	42.2
Netherlands	30.9	26.3	25.4	32.8	31.1	31.4
Norway	10.2	9.0	8.0	9.3	6.9	6.7
Sweden	15.6	16.0	16.4	15.7	16.1	15.2
Other developed areas						
Finland	7.4	5.3	4.8	8.4	7.8	7.7
Greece	6.0	5.0	3.8	5.4	3.4	3.1
Ireland	4.5	2.7	2.4	4.4	2.6	2.5
Spain	18.2	18.3	16.6	17.0	15.2	14.6
Turkey	5.9	4.0	3.4	5.7	3.5	3.2
Yugoslavia	9.5	8.8	8.3	9.1	7.9	7.8
Australia	33.4	34.7	32.4	29.6	25.3	25.3
New Zealand	8.1	5.2	5.1	8.0	5.1	4.9
South Africa	13.0	13.3	11.7	11.2	9.0	7.8

Source: See appendix A.

a. The distribution of SDRs to the developing countries under the link mechanism is proportional to their original shares in SDR allocations (related to their IMF quotas).

b. The distribution of SDRs to the developing countries under the link mechanism is based on LDC shares of total concessional lending from multilateral institutions, 1969–71.

because of its payments weakness after the Smithsonian realignment it is categorized with the payments deficit pressure group, despite its maintenance of parity with gold in December 1971.

Table 3-5 reports the results of the link's net impact on the reserves of advanced countries grouped in these three categories. In general, the hypothesis appears to be borne out: the link does on balance transfer reserves from countries with deficit payments pressure toward those in sur-

Table 3-3. *Effect of an Emission of One Billion SDRs on the Exports of Selected Industrial Countries under 1970–72 and Two Alternative Distributions*
Millions of SDRs

Country	Increase in exports using marginal trade shares			Increase in exports using average trade shares		
	Original	Link A[a]	Link B[b]	Original	Link A[a]	Link B[b]
United States	78.0	193.8	220.9	86.0	213.6	236.6
United Kingdom	22.8	56.6	53.3	29.4	73.0	66.8
Canada	9.0	22.4	19.5	8.4	20.9	23.6
Japan	38.3	95.0	104.6	30.0	74.5	79.4
Industrial Europe						
Austria	1.5	3.8	3.2	1.7	4.2	2.8
Belgium	5.8	14.5	12.7	5.7	14.2	11.3
Denmark	1.9	4.8	4.2	1.7	4.2	3.9
France	16.4	40.6	34.9	16.2	40.4	29.8
Germany	32.7	81.2	74.6	30.0	74.4	73.3
Italy	8.4	20.9	16.6	11.8	29.2	25.0
Netherlands	5.5	13.6	12.7	7.4	18.3	18.7
Norway	2.0	4.9	3.9	1.1	2.8	2.6
Sweden	4.1	10.2	10.6	4.2	10.3	9.4
Other developed areas						
Finland	0.8	1.9	1.5	1.8	4.5	4.4
Greece	1.0	2.5	1.3	0.4	1.0	0.6
Ireland	0.2	0.6	0.3	0.2	0.5	0.4
Spain	4.6	11.5	9.8	3.4	8.4	7.8
Turkey	0.5	1.3	0.7	0.3	0.7	0.5
Yugoslavia	2.0	5.0	4.6	1.7	4.1	4.1
Australia	9.1	22.6	20.3	5.3	13.2	13.1
New Zealand	0.6	1.5	1.3	0.5	1.3	1.2

Source: See appendix A.

a. The distribution of SDRs to the developing countries under a link mechanism is proportional to their original shares in SDR allocations (related to their IMF quotas).

b. The distribution of SDRs to the developing countries under the link mechanism is based on LDC shares of total concessional lending from multilateral institutions, 1969–71.

plus. However, the magnitudes involved appear to be quite small. A total SDR emission of 1 billion raises reserves of the surplus group by only 49 million SDRs, reducing those of the deficit group by 35 million (under the quota-based link using marginal import shares). Since the 1970–72 allocation involved approximately 3 billion SDRs a year, it would appear that the existence of a link would have redirected annually approximately 147 million SDRs toward the surplus group and 105 million SDRs away from the deficit group during the period. These magnitudes would have con-

Table 3-4. *Effect of an Emission of One Billion SDRs on the Reserves and Imports of Selected Developing Countries under 1970–72 and Two Alternative Distributions*

Thousands of SDRs

Country	Reserves			Imports		
	Original	*Link A*[a]	*Link B*[b]	*Original*	*Link A*[a]	*Link B*[b]
Latin America						
Argentina	291	723	406	17,706	43,975	24,697
Bolivia	16	39	91	1,495	3,712	8,525
Brazil	181	449	485	17,817	44,249	47,804
Chile	74	184	100	6,382	15,849	8,600
Colombia	51	127	156	6,369	15,818	19,353
Costa Rica	5	13	21	1,293	3,212	5,391
Dominican Republic	11	28	55	1,700	4,222	8,388
Ecuador	15	36	159	1,307	3,247	14,251
El Salvador	19	46	135	1,362	3,383	9,847
Guatemala	16	40	16	1,388	3,448	1,388
Jamaica	22	54	53	2,067	5,134	5,028
Mexico	156	387	406	14,502	36,016	37,811
Panama	30	76	147	1,433	3,559	6,926
Peru	45	111	168	4,735	11,759	17,701
Trinidad and Tobago	9	23	23	2,446	6,074	6,171
Uruguay	99	247	165	2,721	6,758	4,525
Venezuela	244	605	518	13,010	32,310	27,693
Middle East						
Egypt	60	148	91	7,635	18,962	11,717
Iran	43	106	43	7,263	18,037	7,263
Iraq	60	150	60	2,678	6,650	2,678
Israel	77	191	77	4,974	12,354	4,974
Syria	18	45	18	1,988	4,938	1,988
Asia						
Afghanistan	42	104	135	1,469	3,648	4,742
Burma	103	255	103	2,352	5,842	2,352
Cambodia (Khmer Republic)	12	29	40	1,227	3,048	4,191
India	587	1,457	2,086	37,910	94,152	134,763
Indonesia	37	92	187	10,608	26,346	53,838
Korea	36	89	122	2,584	6,418	8,855
Malaysia	154	383	162	6,998	17,379	7,364
Pakistan and Bangladesh	90	223	345	9,540	23,694	36,585
Philippines	44	109	47	6,034	14,986	6,405
Sri Lanka	25	61	57	3,988	9,904	9,191
Thailand	137	341	137	3,226	8,013	3,226
Vietnam, Republic of	39	98	52	2,297	5,706	3,033
Africa						
Algeria	84	209	84	4,672	11,603	4,672
Ghana	40	100	78	3,512	8,722	6,840
Ivory Coast	13	32	13	1,675	4,159	1,675
Kenya	25	61	70	1,816	4,511	5,137
Morocco	35	86	43	4,592	11,403	5,705
Nigeria	39	96	39	5,343	13,269	5,343
Senegal	8	20	22	1,337	3,321	3,568
Sudan	22	55	22	2,917	7,243	2,917
Tanzania, United Republic of	20	49	80	1,668	4,143	6,843
Tunisia	10	25	31	1,725	4,284	5,443
Uganda	17	43	61	1,623	4,031	5,693
Zaire	47	117	47	4,579	11,372	4,579
Zambia	68	169	68	2,835	7,041	2,835

Source: See appendix A.

a. The distribution of SDRs to the developing countries under the link mechanism is proportional to their original shares in SDR allocations (related to their IMF quotas).

b. The distribution of SDRs to the developing countries under the link mechanism is based on LDC shares of total concessional lending from multilateral institutions, 1969–71.

Table 3-5. *Estimated Impact of the SDR Aid Link on Payments Imbalances among Developed Countries*

| Country | Percentage change in exchange rate relative to the dollar, Smithsonian realignment (December 1971) | Reserves at end of 1971 (billions of SDRs) | Net change in reserves[a] (in millions of SDRs) relative to change under actual distribution using | | | |
| | | | Link A[b] | | Link B[c] | |
			Marginal trade shares	Average trade shares	Marginal trade shares	Average trade shares
Surplus countries						
Belgium	11.57	3.2	−2.6	−2.8	−4.4	−5.6
Germany	13.58	17.2	19.3	15.3	12.7	14.1
Netherlands	11.57	3.5	−4.6	−1.8	−5.5	−1.4
Japan	16.88	14.1	36.5	24.2	46.1	29.1
Total	...	38.0	48.6	34.8	48.9	36.2
Intermediate countries						
Austria	6.22	2.2	−1.9	−1.6	−2.4	−3.0
Denmark	7.45	0.7	−1.6	−2.0	−2.2	−2.3
France	8.57	7.6	−1.8	−2.0	−7.6	−12.5
Italy	7.48	6.3	−4.6	0.3	−8.9	−3.9
Norway	7.49	1.1	−1.2	−2.4	−2.2	−2.6
Sweden	7.49	1.0	0.3	0.4	0.8	−0.5
Ireland	8.57	0.9	−1.8	−1.8	−2.0	−1.9
Spain	8.57	3.0	0.1	−1.7	−1.7	−2.4
Turkey	7.14	0.7	−1.9	−2.3	−2.5	−2.6
Australia	8.57	3.1	1.3	−4.3	−1.0	−4.3
New Zealand	8.57	0.3	−2.9	−3.0	−3.0	−3.1
Finland	2.44	0.7	−2.2	−0.6	−2.6	−0.7
Total	...	27.6	−18.2	−21.0	−35.3	−39.7
Deficit countries						
United Kingdom	8.57	6.1	−20.4	−10.6	−23.6	−16.7
United States	0.00	12.1	−7.7	4.1	19.4	27.1
Canada	0.00	5.3	−5.9	−6.8	−8.9	−4.1
Greece	0.00	0.5	−1.0	−1.9	−2.2	−2.2
Yugoslavia	−11.76	0.2	−0.7	−1.3	−1.2	−1.3
South Africa	−4.76	0.7	0.3	−2.3	−1.3	−3.5
Total	...	24.9	−35.4	−18.7	−17.8	−0.7

Sources: Calculated from International Monetary Fund, *International Financial Statistics*, selected issues and table 3-2.

a. For an emission of 1 billion SDRs.

b. The distribution of SDRs to the developing countries under the link mechanism is proportional to their original shares in SDR allocations (related to their IMF quotas).

c. The distribution of SDRs to the developing countries under the link mechanism is based on LDC shares of total concessional lending from multilateral institutions, 1969–71.

stituted only a 0.39 percent increment a year in total reserves for the surplus group and a 0.42 percent decline for the deficit group (which stood at $38.0 billion and $24.9 billion, respectively, at the end of 1971).

Various other aspects of the reserve impact calculations warrant attention. The increases attributable to a link are concentrated in two countries: Germany and Japan. This is not surprising given the strong competitive stance of the two countries during the period. The results for the United States are somewhat more surprising: despite its serious deficit position, the estimates indicate only a small reserve loss for the United

States using the quota-based link, marginal trade share variant, and increases in reserves in the other three variants calculated. Reserve losses attributable to a link are consistently registered for the other deficit group countries, however, especially in the cases of the United Kingdom and Canada.

The use of average rather than marginal trade shares provides a check indicating that for most countries the marginal share calculations are of reasonable magnitudes. As expected, the average trade shares generate smaller amounts of reserve gains by surplus countries and losses by deficit countries than the marginal shares, which are more indicative of the direction of change in trade in the base period.

Using the multilateral lending agency link (link B), reserve gains for surplus countries are almost identical to those under the quota-based link (with Japan gaining and Germany losing), but the reserve losses of the deficit group are smaller (especially when average rather than marginal trade shares are used). This result is caused primarily by the higher weight of India, Indonesia, and Pakistan in the multilateral lending agency variant, combined with the high U.S. share in these countries' imports in the trade pattern estimation period (1967–71).

In all four cases (that is, two link variants using two trade pattern variants each) the combined reserve losses of the intermediate and deficit groups exceed the gains of the surplus group. This result follows from the existence of SDR leakage into LDC reserves under a link, even though this leakage is quite small.

In sum, the empirical simulations indicate that although the "payments imbalance aggravation" effect of a link is verified, the magnitude of the effect is clearly too small to warrant concern.

Effect of a Link on Inflation: Results

The simulations also lend themselves to examination of another major drawback that has been cited for a link: the inflationary impact. Any reasonable figures for aid given under a link mechanism compared with the aggregate GNP of the industrial countries indicate that this effect too would be inconsequential. However, it is useful to examine the effect explicitly, considering the incidence of a link on export demand. In the inflationary climate of the early 1970s, there has been heightened concern about the inflationary impact on the domestic economy of increases in exports (and hence reductions in domestic availability of goods), with the most spectacular instances in agriculture and involving formal or informal export quotas.

The impact of a 1 billion SDR emission on the exports of developed countries reported in table 3-3 may be translated into an evaluation of the net impact of a link on export demand. The calculations for this examination use a 3 billion SDR emission (the annual rate in the first allocation period), and the results are compared with the mid-period annual exports of goods and services from the industrial countries. The results of this exercise are shown in table 3-6. The net increment in export demand resulting from either of the alternative links is trivial compared with pre-existing export levels in developed countries. Considering the maximum net export impact estimates for the United States, Germany, and Japan, these results indicate that a link could have added to export demand in the respective amounts of only 0.65 percent, 0.30 percent, and 0.69 percent, respectively. Even with very inelastic export supply, these increments could not have generated significant inflationary pressure in the advanced countries.

TO RECAPITULATE, the simulations of this section afford a detailed assessment of the impact of an SDR aid link on the reserves and exports of advanced countries. The possibly deleterious influence of a link through aggravation of payments imbalances (by channeling respent reserves toward surplus and away from deficit countries) is found to be directionally accurate but of inconsequential magnitude, as is the inflationary impact of a link operating through the resulting increase in demand for advanced country exports.

IMF Gold Sales through a Trust Fund

On August 31, 1975, the Interim Committee of the IMF Board of Governors on the International Monetary System announced an agreement advocating the sale of one-sixth of the IMF's gold for the benefit of the developing countries and the restitution of one-sixth of the Fund's gold to members.[64] Profits on the sale of gold arising from the difference between the market price and the former official price would be used for aid to the developing countries.[65]

64. International Monetary Fund, *IMF Survey*, September 15, 1975, p. 265.
65. The announcement stated that "the proportion of any profits or surplus value

Table 3-6. *Estimated Net Impact of the SDR Aid Link on Export Demand of Selected Industrial Countries, SDR Emission of Three Billion SDRs*
Millions of SDRs

| | | Net increase in export demand using | | | |
| | | Link A[a] | | Link B[b] | |
Industrial country	Exports of goods and services, 1971	Marginal trade shares	Average trade shares	Marginal trade shares	Average trade shares
United States	69,249	347	383	429	452
United Kingdom	33,630	101	131	92	110
Canada	22,067	40	37	32	46
Japan	28,406	170	134	199	148
Industrial Europe					
Austria	4,989	7	7	5	3
Belgium	14,205	26	25	21	17
Denmark	4,955	9	7	7	7
France	28,087	73	72	56	41
Germany	48,222	146	133	126	130
Italy	21,555	37	52	25	40
Netherlands	17,243	24	33	22	34
Norway	5,108	9	5	6	4
Sweden	9,097	18	18	20	16
Other developed areas					
Finland	3,011	3	8	2	8
Greece	1,432	5	2	1	1
Ireland	1,731	1	1	0	1
Spain	5,950	21	15	16	13
Turkey	1,366	2	1	1	0
Yugoslavia	3,391	9	7	8	7
Australia	6,186	40	24	34	23
New Zealand	1,579	3	2	2	2
South Africa	4,329	15	7	10	4

Sources: International Monetary Fund, *Balance of Payments Yearbook, 1971*, and table 3-3.
   a. The distribution of SDRs to the developing countries under the link mechanism is proportional to their original shares in SDR allocations (related to their IMF quotas).
   b. The distribution of SDRs to the developing countries under the link mechanism is based on LDC shares of total concessional lending from multilateral institutions, 1969–71.

At the Jamaica meetings in January 1976 the Interim Committee agreed to the immediate implementation of the earlier agreement on gold and added important details on the measures proposed. Profits from the

of the gold sold for the benefit of developing countries that would correspond to the share of quotas of these countries would be transferred directly to each developing country in proportion to its quota." (Ibid.)

sale of gold would be channeled through a trust fund, which should be augmented by voluntary contributions. Aid through the trust fund would be limited to countries with per capita incomes below 300 SDR in 1973. The sale of one-sixth of the IMF's gold, or 25 million ounces, would be phased over a period of four years.[66]

The idea of establishing a trust fund financed by profits on sales of some portion of the IMF's holdings of gold was contained in a proposal made by the United States in December 1974. That proposal also provided for direct contributions to the trust fund by oil-exporting countries and other countries in a position to contribute. The proposal initially met resistance from countries opposed to the sale of gold, particularly France. The compromise agreement reached on August 31, 1975, contained two provisions attractive to the opposing countries: (1) half of the gold released by the IMF would be returned directly to member countries; and (2) by a parallel agreement, central banks would now be permitted to carry out transactions in gold using prices other than the artificially low "official price"—though it was ambiguous whether the latter provision could be effective at once or only after formal amendment of the IMF Articles of Agreement.[67]

Although the establishment of a trust fund has now been agreed upon, the limitations of this new source for development assistance should be kept in mind. Assuming a market price on the order of $125.00 an ounce, the sale of 25 million ounces would provide profits of approximately $2 billion. This aid would be spread over four years; a more accelerated scheduling of the gold sales would run a greater risk of depressing the market price of gold, thereby reducing the amount of aid possible through this mechanism.[68] The resulting annual flow of $500 million in aid would be very modest compared with total flows of concessional assistance.[69]

66. Communiqué of the Interim Committee as reported in *IMF Survey,* January 19, 1976, p. 18.

67. Further details of the agreements on the treatment of gold are discussed in chapter 4, pages 99–100.

68. Indeed, between August 28, 1975, before the first announcement of the agreement, and January 15, 1976, one week after its confirmation in Jamaica, the price of gold on the London market fell from $161.70 to $132.50 an ounce. Some or most of this decline may reasonably be attributed to the prospect of the IMF gold sales for the trust fund. Note that the 25 million ounces of gold represent approximately two-thirds of the average annual world production of gold outside the USSR in recent years. (Calculated from *International Financial Statistics,* July 1974.)

69. Preliminary data indicate a total of $11.3 billion in concessional "official de-

Despite its limited magnitude, aid resulting from IMF gold sales should play a significant role because it will be focused on the poorest developing countries (though its impact would be all the greater if it were matched by contributions to the trust fund by oil-exporting countries, as suggested in the initial proposal by the United States). In addition, it will come at a time of great need because of the increased burden of the cost of imported oil. Finally, the instrument itself contains the possibility of more aid in the future: IMF members could decide to use some or all of the remaining two-thirds of the IMF's gold for the same purpose, and the requirement of restitution to members of one-half of that gold could be eliminated in future operations of this type.

At the IMF and World Bank annual meetings in September 1975, and again in Jamaica in January 1976, most developing countries welcomed the Interim Committee's agreement on gold sales. However, some representatives of developing countries expressed dissatisfaction over the corresponding agreement to permit gold transactions among central banks at prices other than the official price.[70] These delegates held that the changes in the treatment of gold were likely to increase world liquidity by large amounts through an effective rise in the price of gold reserves. The result of this increase in liquidity could be the creation of fewer SDRs in the future, which would be detrimental to the LDCs even if there were no link between SDRs and aid—since the share of the developing countries in world gold reserves (9 percent) is far below their share in SDRs (approximately one-fourth). The shortcoming of this argument is that it fails to recognize that the economic value of gold reserves had already been raised above their valuation at a low "official" price, as discussed in chapter 4. The IMF gold sales and trust fund at least will obtain some aid benefit for the LDCs from the fait accompli of higher effective liquidity of official gold holdings caused by the increase in the market price of gold.

EVEN THOUGH aid from profits on IMF gold sales, channeled through a trust fund, will be more an ad hoc mechanism than a permanent feature of a revised international monetary system, the instrument should provide

---

velopment assistance," by OECD donors in the July 1974–June 1975 period. (*IMF Survey,* August 25, 1975, p. 248.)

70. (*IMF Survey,* September 15, 1975, p. 270.) The critique was reiterated in the formal statement of the Group of Twenty-Four developing countries at the Jamaica meeting. (*IMF Survey,* January 19, 1976, p. 28.)

important concessional assistance to the poorest LDCs in paying the higher oil prices. More aid in the future could come from sales of part of the remaining IMF gold, expecially if there were no requirement of restitution of gold to IMF members. In any event the establishment of the mechanism does not preclude a future SDR aid link.[71]

Summary Assessment

Any evaluation of proposals to link SDRs to aid must first consider the relevant magnitudes of trade, aid, and linked aid. In 1973 developing countries received approximately $136 billion in foreign exchange from exports of goods, services, and net private capital inflow.[72] Official development assistance (for 1972) was $8.7 billion.[73] A link based on 1970–72 levels of SDR emissions might generate $1 billion in aid annually, before deducting any induced reduction in aid passing through other channels. With a grant component of linked aid of 50 percent, the annual net welfare gain would be $500 million. If the shadow price of foreign exchange in the LDCs were on the average one-third above the market price, the $136 billion in market-based foreign exchange receipts would represent an annual net welfare gain of $45 billion. Hence, the welfare gain to the LDCs that might result from a link, even with optimistic assumptions, would amount to approximately 1½ percent of the

71. Even though it may well be true that the proposal for gold sales and a trust fund reduced pressure for the adoption of a link at the present time. In this connection it is worth noting that the intensity of the LDC demand for a link seems to have abated after the meeting of the Interim Committee in January 1975. In the communiqué of that meeting, the section dealing with the agenda for amendments to the Articles of Agreement (paragraph 6.I) excluded mention of a link, which was referred to in a separate section (6.II) with the note that "there continues to be a diversity of views on this matter. It was agreed to keep the matter under active study. . . ." (*IMF Survey*, January 20, 1975, pp. 18–19.) This meeting of the Interim Committee followed soon after the original U.S. proposal on gold sales and the trust fund.

72. Merchandise exports were $100 billion (International Monetary Fund, *International Financial Statistics* [IMF, selected issues]). Service exports were approximately $25 billion based on past relationships (International Monetary Fund, *Balance of Payments Yearbook* [IMF, selected issues]), and net private capital flows (using 1972 data) were $11 billion (Edwin M. Martin, *Development Co-operation: Efforts and Policies of the Members of the Development Assistance Committee* [OECD, 1973]).

73. Ibid.

welfare gain already attained through trade and capital flows.[74] There-fore, if the creation of a link had negative side effects causing a reduction of 1½ percent or more in the levels of world trade and capital flows other-wise attainable, then the linked aid would be canceled out by LDC losses in welfare due to a decline in exports and capital flows. Examination of the various economic arguments indicates that it would be unlikely that a link itself would do even this amount of damage to the world trading and capital flow system. However, it seems quite probable that failure to agree upon international monetary reform measures because of intransigence over the link issue on either side could do this much damage and more.

Another basic consideration is the hard reality that no SDRs may be created whatsoever for a number of years. The above comparison of a link and "market" welfare gains assumes SDR emissions on the scale of the first emission period, but at present there are no SDR emissions. The recent explosive growth in world reserves, including the implicit monetiza-tion of gold at a higher price, make it doubtful that additional SDRs will be created for some years. Thus the benefits of a link, even if one were agreed upon, could very well prove to be nonexistent for a number of years; the link could bestow on the LDCs an increased share in nothing.

A third general consideration involves the bargaining strategy of de-veloped and developing countries on monetary reform. The original posi-tion of the LDCs was that they would block any agreement on reform of the international monetary system without provision for an aid link. This position may be examined in terms of simple game theory. Consider the payoff matrix of net benefits in three alternative situations, shown below.

	Net benefits with		
	No reform	*Reform with a link*	*Reform without a link*
Developed countries	$D1$	$D2$	$D3$
Developing countries	$L1$	$L2$	$L3$

For the LDCs rationally to oppose reform without a link, one of two situations must be true:

(a) $L1 > L3$; or (b) $\{[(D2 - D1)/D1] \div [(L3 - L1)/L1]\} > C^*$

where C^* is some sufficiently high ratio (exceeding unity). In other words, either (a) the LDCs would be worse off under a reformed system with no

---

74. After applying the shadow price to the $500 million link aid as well (since it would arrive in foreign exchange equivalent).

link than they would be in the complete absence of reform, or (b) the LDCs would have relatively little to gain from a reformed system with no link whereas the developed countries would have a great deal to gain from reform, even after allowance for a link, and the LDCs could exploit this situation to threaten disruption of the industrial countries' potential gains, at little cost to themselves.

The considerations on welfare gains from world trade and capital flows, discussed above, suggest that case (a) is not applicable: the LDCs cannot expect their benefits to be greater under an unreformed system than under a reformed system that had no mechanism for linked aid. An evaluation of case (b) is more difficult, but it seems reasonable to expect that the proportional gains of the LDCs under a reformed system would be at least as great as those of the developed countries so that the condition of a favorable "disruption threat potential"—or a high ratio in (b) —would not be met.[75] In view of the fact that the LDCs did not block the agreements of the Interim Committee meetings in Jamaica (especially the key agreement on flexible exchange rates), it would appear that they now have reached the same conclusion as that suggested here: the benefits of the link are not great enough to warrant blocking reform on other major issues.

It should be noted that although the above discussion draws a dichotomy between LDCs and developed countries, several of the industrial countries in fact have in various forums stated their acceptance of one or another form of a link. The most unambiguous and continuous opposition to a link in any form has come from the United States and Germany.

With these considerations in mind, a summary assessment of the link would be the following:

1. The expectations, discussion, and acrimony generated by link proposals have been completely out of proportion to the significance of the instrument itself. On the one hand, the link is likely to generate only very meager incremental grant equivalent aid, considering the facts that (a) very little creation of SDRs is likely to be appropriate over the next few years, given probable world reserve developments; (b) even at the rate of SDR creation in the 1970–72 period, a link would be likely to generate

75. That is, suppose the proportional gains of reform without a link were equal for the developed countries and LDCs, or $D3/D1 = L3/L1$. Then the threat potential ratio (b) would be less than unity, because the numerator applying to the gains of developed countries refers to their gains in the presence of a link, and these gains are less than those in the absence of a link, or $D2/D1 < D3/D1$.

gross aid amounting to only one-eighth of the total aid through alternative channels; (c) the new higher interest rate on the SDR reduces the grant component of link aid; and (d) there would in all probability be some reduction in aid flowing through alternative channels with the justification of arguments that the monetary system would now take care of aid needs. On the other hand, the link would neither benefit nor deter in any substantial degree the workings of the international monetary system and the achievement of price stability under it.

2. As currently proposed by the LDCs, the link would be an inefficient aid instrument, conferring on developing countries already too prosperous for IDA eligibility 40 cents out of every dollar of gross link aid (and thus raising the possibility of a regressive redistribution of net aid funds from poorer to richer LDCs if aid through other channels were cut back). Therefore, if the developed countries do agree to a link, they should insist that it be limited to the poorer LDCs, using a cutoff per capita income similar to that applied by IDA. Moreover, allocation among recipients within even this group should not be based on IMF quotas—which rise per capita as per capita income rises—but on more appropriate measures (for example, population and indicators of policy "performance").[76]

3. The arguments for and against the link on economic grounds (other than with regard to welfare redistribution) are weak. Some are misconceived (SDRs are not a complete windfall that should go to the poor), some are outdated or at least inapplicable for a permanent instrument (world unemployment is not an argument that justifies a link), some dubious but comfortably unverifiable (the confidence issue), and some directionally correct but empirically of negligible importance (inflation and payments imbalance aggravation). Therefore, from an economic efficiency standpoint, whether a link does or does not eventually emerge from the bargaining seems of secondary importance, whereas the principal danger is that intransigence on either side of the issue will forestall agreement on the other basic elements of international monetary reform.

The adoption of a link does not appear urgent even from the standpoint of welfare improvement through wealth redistribution, because it would generate little or no aid in the near future if the assessment is correct that there will be no creation of SDRs during the next few years. At present

76. For such an aid allocation model, see, for example, William R. Cline and Nicholas P. Sargen, "Performance Criteria and Multilateral Aid Allocation," *World Development,* vol. 3 (June 1975), pp. 383–91.

the LDCs can take advantage of the aid from profits on IMF gold sales, and postpone the issue of the link until SDR creation appears more likely (at which time, for an effective welfare impact, the link proposal should be so redesigned that its benefits are limited to the poorest countries).

A final qualification on this assessment is that it is based on likely developments in the next few years. One may ask whether in the longer run an SDR aid link might not be capable of being a much more important source of aid than implied in the above discussion. If the monetary system truly achieved the goal of ending reserve creation through the accumulation (or appreciation) of gold and foreign exchange, then quite substantial annual SDR emissions would become appropriate (after an initial period of adjustment to excessive reserve creation in recent years and probably in the next few years in view of oil exporters' reserve accumulation). For example, a 5 percent annual growth for world reserves based solely on SDRs would involve the creation of approximately 10 billion SDRs. Even so, a transfer of half of the SDR share of developed countries to a link would generate only about 3.5 billion SDRs a year, which would be relatively modest in relation to overall aid and capital flows to the LDCs to be anticipated in the late 1970s. If such aid from a link were concentrated in the very poor fourth world, its impact in terms of world welfare might nevertheless be considerable. If dissipated among the more prosperous LDCs in proportion to IMF quotas, even this benefit would be reduced.

CHAPTER FOUR

The Adequacy of World Reserves

ANY EVALUATION OF THE MECHANISMS to link the creation of Special Drawing Rights to development assistance must include an assessment of the adequacy of world reserves and the likelihood that SDRs will be created at all during the next few years. Moreover, the existence of flexible rather than fixed rates affects the requirements for world reserves. It is therefore useful to consider briefly the question of the adequacy of world reserves, given its important relationships to the two central topics of this study: LDC interests in exchange rate flexibility and the SDR aid link.

Influence of Flexible Exchange Rates

Traditionally, fixed exchange rates have been considered to require more reserves than flexible rates. Fluctuations in the balance of payments would be taken care of by compensatory exchange rate adjustments under a flexible regime, whereas they involve temporary swings in reserve holdings under a fixed regime. With flexible rates, fundamental disequilibria would be more promptly corrected, because the correct changes in price signals to exporters and importers would occur more quickly than under fixed rates held constant for too long. However, in a system of floating rates managed by monetary authorities, governments still intervene to "lean against the wind" in an effort to maintain the exchange rates close to perceived long-run equilibrium levels, so that they need reserves to intervene when necessary. Nevertheless, with no commitment to maintain

96

a target exchange rate at all costs, the amount of reserves required under flexible rates ought to be reduced. If managed, flexible exchange rates are generally adopted, there should be a decline in the requirements for world reserves.

A recent theoretical analysis by Makin[1] concludes that the elasticity of demand for precautionary reserves with respect to the width of the "band" allowed for fluctuation around a central rate is between -0.3 and -0.5. That is, an increase of the width of the band by 10 percent (for example) permits a reduction of between 3 percent and 5 percent in the level of reserves. This result indicates that reserve needs are highly sensitive to increased flexibility. Using the conservative end of this range (elasticity of -0.3) it is instructive to consider the implied reduction in the need for reserves based on experience with floating to date. Before 1973, the bands of fluctuation allowed by the International Monetary Fund were 2¼ percent on each side of the central rates.[2] During the period of floating rates since 1973, three major countries have maintained their effective exchange rates within the following bands (either by intervention or because of market forces): Germany, 3 percent; France, 7 percent; United States, 6 percent.[3] From a base of 2¼ percent, these wider bands under "floating rates" imply the following percentage reductions in required precautionary reserves: Germany, 10 percent; France, 63 percent; United States, 50 percent.[4] Although these figures are merely illustrative, they

1. John H. Makin, "Exchange Rate Flexibility and the Demand for International Reserves," *Weltwirtschaftliches Archiv,* vol. 110, no. 2 (1974), pp. 229–43. Makin's analysis builds on the "square root law" for reserves—the proposition, based on statistical theory, that the optimal real reserves level increases only as the square root of the real level of trade. That theory in turn justifies a declining rather than constant reserves-imports ratio over time.

2. Note that these bands themselves had been increased from 1 percent at the time of the Smithsonian agreement to realign exchange rates.

3. Calculated from monthly averages of "effective" or "trade-weighted" exchange rates for July 1973 through April 1975, as reported by Morgan Guaranty Trust Company of New York, *World Financial Markets,* monthly issues.

4. That is, the reduction equals 0.3 times the percentage increase in the band; for example, the increase in band for Germany is 33 percent, the decrease in needed reserves is 9.9 percent. Note that the calculation is somewhat biased toward overstating the reduction in needed reserves for nondollar currencies, because their base period band is stated relative to the central rate and hence relative to the dollar, allowing a larger effective band vis-à-vis all other currencies, and hence a larger band for the effective exchange rate. This bias goes in the opposite direction from the bias introduced by considering the 2¼ percent band as the fixed-rate period base, rather than the 1 percent band in effect before December 1971.

suggest that the theoretically justified level for world reserves should have declined by very substantial proportions under the new regime of floating rates.

Although most economists would probably agree that a move to flexible exchange rates should reduce reserve needs (but not necessarily by the magnitudes computed above), this opinion is not unanimous. Harrod has argued that under flexible rates the need for reserves would increase. Authorities would still need to intervene but they would no longer have at their disposal the powerful instrument of monetary policy to attract or repel short-term capital inflow, because the risk of uncertain exchange rates would inhibit the flow of capital in response to interest differentials. Therefore, he concludes, reserves necessary to smooth fluctuations would be greater under flexible than under fixed rates.[5] Another consideration, primarily relevant to the developing countries, is that countries attempting to peg their currencies to those of industrial countries could require larger reserves if the rates of industrial countries were floating than if they were fixed. Movements in the "center" country's exchange rate vis-à-vis third countries could be inappropriate for the developing country pegging its exchange rate to that of the center country.

THERE ARE arguments for both increased and decreased needs of world reserves after a move to flexible rates. The majority view—that reserve needs should decline—seems the more valid, which suggests that total world reserve requirements under the present regime of floating should be lower than they were under the fixed-rate regime before 1973.

Gold Prices

The London market price of gold rose from $39.90 an ounce at the end of June 1971 to $144.00 an ounce in mid-1974, while the official price moved only from $35.00 an ounce to $42.22 an ounce.[6] To evaluate the adequacy of world reserves it is therefore fundamental to decide whether the official or market price should be used in evaluating gold reserves. Using the official price, total world reserves of gold stood at $43 billion

5. Roy Forbes Harrod, *Reforming the World's Money* (London: Macmillan, 1965), pp. 45–49.
6. See table 4-1.

in mid-1974; at the market price, their value was $147 billion. The difference was more than 50 percent of total official world reserves in mid-1974 ($203 billion). If the market gold price is the relevant valuation, the reasonable conclusion is that world reserves are excessive rather than scarce, and that there is no need to create more SDRs.

There is no doubt that the proper price for evaluating gold reserves should be above the official price of $44.22 an ounce, and indeed the IMF Interim Committee on the International Monetary System agreed on August 31, 1975, to abolish the official price. The same agreement eliminated the restriction that had prohibited central banks from making transactions in gold at prices other than the official price; it committed the participants to refrain from pegging the price of gold; and the Group of Ten participants in the agreement agreed that the total stock of gold held by the IMF and by themselves would not be increased.[7]

Even before the Interim Committee's agreement on changes in the treatment of gold, authorities could in effect make transactions with other central banks at a price related to the market price, by contracting loans guaranteed with gold as collateral.[8] After the August 31, 1975, agreement on gold it seems even more certain that the appropriate value for gold reserves is at a price well above the old official price. Central banks will be able to sell gold directly to other central banks, the most natural source of demand. To be sure, attempts to sell large amounts would risk depressing the price. Many central banks may be reluctant to purchase gold because of the risk involved, especially in view of the official commitment to abstain from pegging the price of gold. Nevertheless, even with a dis-

7. International Monetary Fund, *IMF Survey,* September 15, 1975, p. 263. Note that there is disagreement on whether central banks can buy gold at the market price prior to formal amendment of the IMF Articles of Agreement; the IMF says they cannot, but some members, especially France, maintain that the relevant sections of the existing Articles prohibiting purchases at other than official prices no longer have legal force, because the par value system they were meant to support no longer exists. The dispute should be only temporary, since within one or two years formal amendment of the Articles should be complete.

8. Germany made such a loan to Italy for $2 billion in August 1974 with the valuation of the gold collateral reportedly set at 80 percent of the prevailing free market price (*New York Times,* September 1, 1974). In June 1974 the Group of Ten agreed to permit loans with gold collateral to be made among central banks with valuation of the gold at prices other than the official price. (International Monetary Fund, *Annual Report of the Executive Director for the Fiscal Year Ending April 30, 1974* [IMF, 1974], p. 40.)

count to allow for these factors the appropriate valuation of official gold reserves must be much closer to the market price than to the former official price of $44.22 an ounce.

A PROPER ECONOMIC evaluation of the supply of world reserves requires that gold be valued at a price somewhat below its market price but far above the official price, which in any case is to be abolished. This fact, combined with the other influences on world reserves discussed in this chapter, suggests that world reserves are ample and that there is little case for the creation of additional liquidity through the emission of new SDRs.

Finally, the effective rise in world liquidity caused by the rise in gold's market price has not been neutral with regard to the distribution of reserves. The share of the developing countries in gold reserves is only 9 percent, far below their one-fourth share in Special Drawing Rights. Thus effective liquidity created by a rise in the real economic value of gold rather than by an expansion of SDRs imposes a relative loss on the LDCs (even without a link for SDRs). Hence, the market behavior of gold has dealt a double blow to the LDCs: it has left them relatively behind in the expansion of effective reserves, and it has also deprived them of new SDRs by reducing or eliminating the need to create SDRs to achieve adequate world liquidity.

World Reserves and the Oil Price Rise

The precipitous rise in the price of oil in 1973–74 will undoubtedly swell world reserves. The increased annual current account surplus of the oil-exporting countries was estimated to be $60 billion in 1974,[9] although the surplus is likely to be much less in 1975 and will probably decline still further over time as imports of the petroleum-exporting countries grow and as oil-consuming countries reduce their consumption and increase their own production of oil. The surplus could be drastically reduced if the cartel of the Organization of Petroleum Exporting Countries broke and a steep decline occurred in the price of oil, although this possibility seems unlikely.

Two steps are needed to evaluate the effect of this massive new surplus of OPEC members on SDR creations. The first step is to determine its

9. IMF, *Annual Report* (1974), p. 24.

effect on world reserves, and the second step is to examine the likely response of IMF members in decisions about SDR creation given the change in those reserves. Ironically, the oil countries' new surpluses theoretically can lead to increases, decreases, or no change in aggregate world reserves. There would be no change if the oil exporters turned their receipts into assets that duplicate those out of which oil-importing countries drew down their own reserves to pay for the oil. There could even be a decline in world reserves if European countries and Japan used their accumulated dollar balances to pay for OPEC oil, and the OPEC members then used the receipts to buy securities in the United States that do not qualify for "reserve" status (for example, corporate stocks). The most likely result, however, will be a rise in world reserves nearly equaling the magnitude of the current account surpluses of the oil exporters.

The increase in world reserves occurs in the following way. To pay for oil, a European country, for example, borrows dollars in the Eurodollar market. By borrowing, the importing country avoids reducing its reserves. However, the exporting OPEC country deposits these dollars once again in the Eurodollar market, providing the financing for the loan in the first place—that is, "recycling." The European country's reserves do not fall, and OPEC reserves rise. The result is a net increase in aggregate world reserves equal to the rise in the current account surplus of the oil-exporting countries.[10]

In short, although in principle the oil price rise could increase or decrease world reserves, it is reasonable to assume that the actual result will be to increase global reserves as traditionally measured by an amount close to the "oil deficit" of the non-OPEC countries.[11] This result is the more certain because payments by the United States and the United Kingdom for their own oil imports directly increase foreign exchange reserves even if immediately placed again in the United States and the United Kingdom (unless placed in assets not having reserve status).[12]

Thus it is likely that during the next few years world reserves will rise by very substantial amounts due to the oil price increase. This source of re-

10. A discussion of the mechanics of reserve changes resulting from the oil price rise is given in IMF, *Annual Report* (1974), pp. 40–41.

11. Ibid. Note that actual experience in calendar year 1974 was that world reserves rose by an amount ($38 billion) very close to the rise in the oil-importing countries' reserves ($32.5 billion). (International Monetary Fund, *International Financial Statistics* [April 1975], pp. 20–26.)

12. The same phenomenon for such "reserve center" importers will also apply to other countries whose currencies oil exporters may choose to hold as reserves.

serve growth might approximate $30 billion to $50 billion yearly (in view of the $60 billion current account surplus estimated for oil exporters in 1974). In comparison with the total stock of world reserves, increases of this dimension would be extremely large.[13]

If oil-surplus reserves followed this path and if world liquidity needs were assessed in relation to the simple total of world reserves, it would be very difficult to justify creating additional liquidity through new SDR emissions over the next few years. However, there is a strong case for considering OPEC reserves separately from those of the rest of the world. Concern about overexpansion of world reserves must refer to concern about inflation generated by the increased demand induced by expansion of the international monetary base. Yet the OPEC reserves will be essentially excess reserves: sterilized, idle balances that do not lead to a rapid increase in purchases by the oil-exporting countries. (Indeed, in terms of Keynesian demand analysis the oil price rise is recessionary rather than inflationary—aside from the direct initial impact on the oil component of the price indexes—because it siphons off purchasing capacity and reduces nonoil demand.) To the extent that these reserves remain idle and grossly in excess of normal "working" amounts to cover swings in OPEC imports, they are different in economic effect from the reserves of the rest of the world. Therefore, it might be argued that they may appropriately be excluded from the calculation of global reserves with regard to the international monetary base capable of provoking demand expansion.[14] Moreover, if oil exporters' reserves are excluded from the world total, it may even be argued that reserve needs of the rest of the world are increased by the oil price rise, because of increased recourse to foreign borrowing and a resulting need to hedge against the risk of failure to obtain rollover of these borrowings.

Although OPEC reserves require "separate" treatment from other reserves, it would be fallacious to exclude them entirely in assessing global

13. These stood at $222 billion at the end of 1974. (International Monetary Fund, *International Financial Statistics* [IMF, selected issues]). Fried and Schultze expect accumulation of foreign assets of OPEC countries to peak at $150 billion in 1980, athough only a portion of this total would be in reserve assets. Edward R. Fried and Charles L. Schultze, eds., *Higher Oil Prices and the World Economy* (Brookings Institution, 1975), p. 41.

14. In Keynesian terms, OPEC reserves are characterized by a "liquidity trap"; increased supply of reserves to these countries increases their balances but not effective demand. The IMF's annual report for 1974 tends to hold this view. (International Monetary Fund, *Annual Report* [1974], pp. 41–46.)

reserve availability. The oil-exporting countries may be divided into at least two groups—those with substantial potential for industrial and agricultural development and those with little potential. For the latter (including, perhaps, Kuwait and Abu Dhabi), an optimal reserve strategy would be to accumulate some target level of reserves and finance imports by using income from those reserves in addition to current oil revenue. These countries would exchange a physical asset (oil) for financial assets (reserves) to provide income after the exhaustion of oil supplies.

However, the group with developmental potential (for example, Iran, Venezuela, Nigeria, Indonesia, and, probably, Saudi Arabia) would have a very different optimal reserve strategy. Initially, they would accumulate reserves; but later, as soon as consistent with domestic "absorptive capacity" for investment projects, they would spend their excess reserves to import capital equipment and technology to build up their nonoil productive capacity. They would exchange oil for productive physical capital assets—going one step beyond a conversion merely into financial assets because of their broader base of natural and human resources. In short, for this second group reserves would follow an inverse U-shaped pattern over time—first rising but eventually falling as imports from domestic development began to exceed current oil revenue and to eat into reserves accumulated in the interim period.

For this group of OPEC countries capable of domestic development, which probably gain the bulk of oil earnings, it is inaccurate to assume a permanent immobilization of reserves. Instead, it is quite likely that after an interval of time their reserves (as well as their current export earnings) will be spent on imports. Therefore, aside from the problem of phasing over time, their reserves must be characterized as comparable to those of all other countries; that is, their reserves over time should be nonexcess reserves, relevant for the "international monetary base" on which demand (and, potentially, inflation) is based.

After an interim period, the spending of reserves by this group could have an inflationary impact on the world economy. Essentially, the impact would be the same as that associated with any expansion of this magnitude in the international monetary base except that in the OPEC case there would be a delayed reaction after an interim period during which idle reserve balances would be held. However, the very act of spending could once again shrink global reserves if nonoil-exporting countries were to use the resulting improvement in their payments balances to retire the external debt originally incurred to finance oil purchases. Nevertheless, in view of the likely pressures for domestic consumption, it is more probable that the debtor nonoil-producing countries would use their improvement in balance of payments to consume more imports rather than to reduce debt. The total of world reserves would thus remain constant rather than decline.[15]

To RECAPITULATE, the oil price rise has the following implications: global reserves are likely to rise by quite large amounts, approximately equal to the OPEC current account surpluses. However, rapid increases in OPEC reserves are not immediately inflationary since these reserves are essentially idle, excess balances. Eventually, the bulk of these reserves will probably be spent on domestic development projects, causing inflationary pressure on exports from other countries. It follows that, although the full amount of increased OPEC reserves cannot accurately be included in assessing global reserve adequacy, neither can these reserves safely be excluded, given their implications for future OPEC spending.

Whatever the assessment of "world reserve adequacy" for non-OPEC countries after accounting for other factors, there should therefore be some additional upward shift in the world liquidity considered to be already available to account for the OPEC reserve accumulations. However, only some portion of the face value of these OPEC reserves should be included in the world total—to adjust for the fact that a sizable portion will be held, not spent, and that even the remaining portion will be spent only after some years.[16]

15. The linkage between the change in the world reserve base and the real inflationary demand for extra exports to the OPEC countries may be seen as follows. At the time the oil-exporting country spends its reserves on imports, if the industrial country uses the export receipts to liquidate its debt in the Eurodollar market, it will have to do so by raising taxes or by borrowing from its own citizens who received the export earnings. This act of taxation or borrowing reduces domestic demand, making room for the increased export demand of the OPEC countries on a noninflationary basis. If the industrial country does not liquidate its Eurodollar debt, then the receipts of exporters remain in the domestic demand total, and, if the economy is at full employment, inflation will be necessary to harmonize the decreased availability of domestic goods with the same domestic monetary demand for goods. (This formulation assumes the country does not appreciate its currency, which would increase imports and dampen the inflationary pressure by passing it on to other countries.)

16. To determine the appropriate portion of OPEC reserves to be included in assessing the availability of world liquidity, the following procedure might be used. Suppose f is the fraction of OPEC reserves accruing to countries in the group with

Evidence on Reserve Adequacy

World reserves have grown exceedingly rapidly in recent years. During the 1970–74 period, reserves grew at the following annual rates: 18½ percent, 41 percent, 21½ percent, 16 percent, and 20½ percent. The very large surge in 1971 was associated with dollar outflows from the United States. Moreover, these growth rates value gold at the official price; valuation of gold at the market price would make them much higher.

It may be argued that while world reserves have grown rapidly, so has the value of world trade, due chiefly to inflation. This argument is essentially a real bills doctrine, which can justify a spiral inflation mechanism; namely, a rapid expansion in the money supply is justified on grounds that the expansion is necessary to hold constant the "real" money supply after a period of inflation. Subject to this caveat, the ratio of official reserves to imports[17] actually declined for the industrial countries in 1974, as shown in table 4-1. (But the "rest of the world," mainly developing countries, was enjoying a relatively high ratio of reserves to imports, caused by reserve increases associated with high commodity prices and foreign borrowing.)

If gold is valued at the market price, however, even the ratio of reserves to imports for the industrial countries indicates ample or excessive current reserves; this ratio is 37 percent, substantially higher than the ratio in

---

long-run industrial and agricultural development potential. Suppose that it is expected that reserves received today will be spent by these countries over m years in fractions h_i with $\Sigma_{i=1}^m h_i = 1$. Let P be the proportion of the receipts from their extra exports that the industrial countries use to increase their own imports rather than to liquidate outstanding debt originally incurred to pay for the oil. Then if the interest rate available on reserve assets is r, a total accumulation of reserves of R by oil countries in the current year could be considered equivalent to an addition to world reserves generally in the amount:

$$PfR \; \Sigma_{i=1}^m \; [h_i/(1+r)^i].$$

Thus, suppose 70 percent of oil exporters' reserve accumulations go to countries intending to spend for domestic development; that 100 percent of these reserves will be spent exactly in the fifth year; that the interest rate is 8 percent; and that the industrial countries will spend half of the receipts and use the other half to retire debt. For an initial OPEC reserve gain of $R = \$50$ billion, one would then count $(0.5)\,(0.7)$ $(50)\,\{1/(1.08)^5\} = \$11.93$ billion into the current increase in world reserves.

17. More sophisticated measures of reserve needs than the ratio of reserves to imports are of course available, but this measure is probably the best single gauge.

Table 4-1. *Indicators of World Reserve Adequacy, 1971–74*

Monetary values in billions of dollars

Item	1971	1972	1973	1974
Reserves, end of second quarter				
Industrial countries	74.2	103.1	119.8	114.4
Oil exporters	6.9	9.8	12.7	30.0
Rest of world	24.0	34.6	50.5	57.6
Total	105.1	147.5	183.1	201.9
Reserves, end of second quarter, with gold valued at market price[a]				
Industrial countries	78.5	125.7	188.8	201.2
Oil exporters	7.1	10.7	15.5	32.8
Rest of world	24.7	38.1	61.7	71.5
Total	110.2	174.5	265.9	306.1
Imports, CIF				
Industrial countries	235.6	281.1	385.9	543.7
Oil exporters	12.9	15.4	21.5	35.1[b]
Rest of world	80.9	88.8	122.0	191.7[b]
Total	329.4	385.3	529.4	770.5
Ratio of reserves to imports with gold valued at official price				
Industrial countries	0.315	0.367	0.311	0.210
Oil exporters	0.534	0.637	0.592	0.854
Rest of world	0.297	0.389	0.414	0.300
Total	0.319	0.383	0.346	0.262
Ratio of reserves to imports with gold valued at market price				
Industrial countries	0.333	0.447	0.489	0.370
Oil exporters	0.547	0.695	0.719	0.933
Rest of world	0.305	0.428	0.505	0.373
Total	0.335	0.453	0.502	0.397

Source: International Monetary Fund, *International Financial Statistics*, April 1975.
a. London market price of gold: 1971, $39.90; 1972, $64.50; 1973, $123.25; 1974, $144.25 (reported in *New York Times*, June 30).
b. Estimated.

1971 (a year already characterized by high reserves). The valuation of gold at the market price overstates reserves but it is probably much closer to economic reality than valuation at the official price.

THE EVIDENCE of the 1971–74 period indicates extremely rapid reserve growth and a current level of adequate or ample reserves. Therefore, creation of additional liquidity by the creation of new SDRs appears unwarranted. This conclusion holds even if only the nonoil-exporting countries are considered, after taking into account inflation in import costs on the one hand and increases in the real economic value of gold reserves on the other.

Conclusion

It does not appear that creation of SDRs will be justified in terms of world liquidity needs during the next few years. Total reserve needs should be reduced because of a shift from fixed to floating exchange rates. Reserves are high, especially if gold is valued at or near the market rather than the official price. Reserve growth has been extremely high in recent years. Mushrooming reserves of the oil-exporting countries, although different in economic impact from reserves of other countries because of their "idle balance" nature, must be taken into account at least partially in any reckoning of available world liquidity, in view of the likely expenditure of some of these reserves on future domestic development programs in OPEC countries.

These factors imply that in the short run little would be gained for the LDCs if they succeeded in linking SDRs to aid, because additional SDRs are not likely to be needed for several years.

CHAPTER FIVE

Conclusion

THE DEVELOPING COUNTRIES have a major stake in the successful reform of the international monetary system. The stability and pace of expansion of international trade and capital flows under that system are of
paramount importance to their economic progress. International monetary reform should enable the less developed countries to benefit from
an improved process of balance of payments adjustment among industrial
countries. The improvement could lead to fewer trade barriers and fewer
instances of depressed export markets in those industrial countries that
are pursuing deflationary measures in order to correct payment deficits.
In addition to the specific measure of aid through a trust fund based on
sales of IMF gold, prospective monetary reform measures and those
already negotiated should enable the LDCs to anticipate: (1) a larger
and more dependable flow of untied capital; (2) a better distribution of
increases in reserves (via unlinked Special Drawing Rights) than one resulting either from gold price increases or speculative capital outflows
from the United States; (3) an opportunity to convert foreign exchange
reserves into SDRs; and (4) a more certain, stable, and smoothly expand-
ing international economy (providing a greater export market and therefore greater import capacity for developing countries). By contrast, the
creation of a link between Special Drawing Rights and development assistance is unlikely to produce substantial benefits for the developing
countries.

The principal concerns about the negative effects of greater exchange
rate flexibility among developed countries appear to be unwarranted.
There is no theoretical or empirical basis for the fear that flexibility in
exchange rates of industrial countries will increase commodity price
fluctuation or reduce real commodity prices. The more general fear of

greater uncertainty under flexible exchange rates is founded upon the un-realistic assumption that fixed rates will not change. In reality the choice is between flexible rates with frequent but modest changes and fixed rates that are likely to collapse periodically in much larger realignments. Analysis of risk aversion confirms that in principle the LDCs should sup-port greater rate flexibility among industrial countries because as risk avoiders they should prefer frequent small changes over infrequent large ones. Furthermore, contrary to the popular impression actual measures of variability indicate that exchange rates were slightly more stable during the floating period beginning in March 1973 than they were during the previous fourteen years, when fixed rates and large discrete adjustments were the rule.

Insofar as greater flexibility of exchange rates among industrial coun-tries is crucial to improvement of the balance of payments adjustment mechanism, the LDCs have much to gain from the Jamaica agreement legitimizing exchange rate regimes. The healthier the international climate, the more buoyant will LDC export markets be—and export growth now has redoubled importance to their economies because of the rise in the price of imported oil.

The SDR aid link is another element of international monetary reform to which the LDC representatives have attached primary importance. Their expectations of development assistance through this mechanism are much greater than its probable efficacy. The explosive growth of world reserves in recent years, the anticipated accumulation of very large re-serves by oil-exporting countries (of which some portion will be spent for domestic development programs), the increased expansion of world re-serves by the effective monetization of gold at close to market prices, all point to a protracted period during which no SDRs will be created at all. Therefore, if an additional share in SDRs is conferred on the LDCs as a "link," it will have no base on which to operate over the intermediate time horizon. Even in the longer run, the magnitudes for such aid are likely to be quite modest, and the increase in the SDR's interest rate reduces the grant equivalent benefit of such an aid measure. The political difficulty of establishing a link at all makes it unrealistic to argue that interest charges also would be waived for SDRs channeled to a link and paid in-stead by the industrial countries.

Although the link does not seem to be a strong instrument for pro-viding additional development assistance, neither does it seem to menace the international monetary system, as some opponents maintain. Empirical calculations simulating the impact of SDR emissions under a link indicate that the mechanism would have an imperceptible inflationary effect on the demand for exports of industrial countries, even for those in the strongest competitive positions. Similarly, although the calculations verify the hypothesis that a link would aggravate payments imbalances among the developed countries, because SDRs that would otherwise have gone to deficit industrial countries would be rechanneled to strongly competitive surplus countries, the results show that this effect would be inconsequential in magnitude. The arguments that a link would jeopardize confidence in SDRs, would lead to the creation of inappropriate amounts of SDRs, and would reduce the amount of aid contributed through conventional channels cannot be tested. The issue of confidence in SDRs is losing force with every year of SDR usage and because of recent improvements in the asset.

But although the link might do no serious harm to the monetary system, it is equally true that it would bring it no benefits. The argument that a link would increase world output because, in industrial countries, it would resolve the dilemma of unemployment caused by inconsistent balance of payments surplus targets is irrelevant. It was not true for the postwar period of expansion and inflation, and it remained untrue during the 1974–75 recession, which was not caused by incompatibility of current accounts targets.

The arguments that a link merely confers on LDCs the windfall gains and social savings from a new international monetary mechanism, the SDR, are largely spurious, since essentially the link would be a vehicle for redistribution of existing wealth. Link advocates have given no attention to the question of confining the dimensions of a link to that component of SDR creation that would add demonstrably to real world output, while excluding from the link the remaining portion of SDRs that would act purely as scrip for laying claim to existing resources.

The most serious flaw of the link mechanism proposed by the LDCs in the Committee of Twenty is that it would confer relatively higher per capita benefits on the more prosperous recipients, because its apportionment is based upon the IMF quotas, allowing for a minor gesture of special treatment for a diminutive roster of least developed countries. Moreover, the direct emissions proposed would circumvent any relationship between the amount of aid and country performance. This feature is a noteworthy departure from nearly all past academic and quasi-official proposals, which usually suggested channeling link resources through a development agency such as the International Development Association.

During the course of the four years of monetary reform negotiations culminating in the Jamaica agreement, the LDCs appear to have shifted from their early position that they would block reform agreements that excluded a link. Instead, they participated in the major agreements of the IMF Interim Committee concerning gold (in August 1975) and flexible exchange rates (in January 1976). Their evolution in bargaining strategy represents a realistic evaluation of their prospective gains from overall monetary reform, even without a link, relative to the special benefits they might have hoped to obtain by demanding a link at the risk of jeopardizing the other reform measures (especially since the reforms successfully negotiated included the IMF gold sale mechanism, which would generate aid sooner than a link).

The profound changes in the world economy that are associated with the oil price increases make flexibility of exchange rates among industrial countries of even greater importance than before, because of the greater urgency to accommodate rapid, major shifts in payment flows, and the greater need for buoyant export earnings for LDCs. At the same time, the practical prospects of aid through a link have become even more remote in view of the reduced likelihood that SDRs will need to be created to augment international liquidity. World reserves should be lower following a move to floating rates; economically meaningful reserves have already increased with the rise in the market price of gold; and at least a portion of the sizable increases expected in oil exporters' reserves would have to be included in any accurate assessment of the supply of global liquidity.

The Jamaica agreements have ushered in a new phase in the evolution of the international monetary system. A period of gaining experience with the new arrangements (including those for coordination of floating exchange rates) is now likely to take the place of the previous stage of intense negotiations in the pursuit of changes in the system. While some elements of reform remain unresolved (particularly those concerning the creation, consolidation, and conversion of reserve assets), key elements of a new system are now in place. The developing countries can rightfully claim part of the credit for the successful reform negotiations achieved to date. They have established beyond doubt their right to participate in the reform process; and if some of their particular objectives have proved elusive—notably the SDR aid link—they have attained others, including not only the new instrument of aid from IMF gold sales but also revisions on other issues less central to monetary reform per se (such as maintenance of their shares in IMF quotas despite an increase in shares of oil-exporting countries and a decrease in those of industrial countries, as well as increases in the IMF's funding for compensatory finance). It is encouraging for the prospects of relations between the industrial and developing countries that, despite the emergence in recent years of an atmosphere of confrontation between the two groups of countries, they have managed together to construct some, and perhaps the most important, of the elements of a new international monetary system.

APPENDIX A

Statistical Tables

Table A-1. *Allocation of Special Drawing Rights to Least Developed Countries, by Amount and Percentage of Total Allocation to Less Developed Countries, 1970–72*

Millions of SDRs

Country	Allocation	Percentage of total LDC allocation
Afghanistan	12.8	0.54
Bhutan[a]	0.0	. . .
Botswana	1.6	0.07
Burundi	6.6	0.28
Chad	4.4	0.19
Dahomey	4.4	0.19
Ethiopia[a]	0.0	. . .
Guinea	8.3	0.36
Haiti	6.6	0.28
Laos	4.4	0.19
Lesotho	1.6	0.07
Malawi	5.1	0.22
Maldives[a]	0.0	. . .
Mali	7.5	0.32
Nepal	2.2	0.10
Niger	4.4	0.19
Rwanda	6.6	0.28
Somalia	6.6	0.28
Sudan	24.9	1.06
Sikkim[a]	0.0	. . .
Tanzania, United Republic of	14.3	0.61
Uganda	13.9	0.59
Upper Volta	4.4	0.19
Western Samoa	0.2	0.01
Yemen Arab Republic	2.1	0.09
Least developed countries, total	142.9	6.09
Developing countries, total	2,348.0	100.0

Sources: International Monetary Fund, *International Financial Statistics*, August 1973. List of least developed countries, as defined in United Nations Conference on Trade and Development, 3rd conf., Resolution 62.

a. IMF member but not a participant in the Special Drawing Rights account.

Table A-2. *Ratio of Reserves to Imports of Goods and Services,*
Forty-seven Developing Countries, 1967-71

Country	Ratio of reserves to imports	Country	Ratio of reserves to imports
Latin America		Burma	0.727
Argentina	0.274	Cambodia (Khmer Republic)	0.160
Bolivia	0.177	India	0.258
Brazil	0.169	Indonesia	0.058
Chile	0.193	Korea	0.230
Colombia	0.134	Malaysia	0.367
Costa Rica	0.065	Pakistan and Bangladesh	0.157
Dominican Republic	0.109	Philippines	0.121
Ecuador	0.186	Sri Lanka	0.103
El Salvador	0.228	Thailand	0.709
Guatemala	0.195	Vietnam, Republic of	0.285
Jamaica	0.175	*Africa*	
Mexico	0.179	Algeria	0.300
Panama	0.354	Ghana	0.191
Peru	0.158	Ivory Coast	0.129
Trinidad and Tobago	0.062	Kenya	0.226
Uruguay	0.609	Morocco	0.126
Venezuela	0.312	Nigeria	0.121
Middle East		Senegal	0.101
Egypt	0.130	Sudan	0.126
Iran	0.098	Tanzania, United Republic of	0.196
Iraq	0.376	Tunisia	0.096
Israel	0.257	Uganda	0.178
Syria	0.151	Zaire	0.172
Asia		Zambia	0.400
Afghanistan	0.473		

Sources: 1966–70, end-of-year reserves, International Monetary Fund, *International Financial Statistics* (August 1973); divided by 1967–71 average imports of goods and services, International Monetary Fund, *Balance of Payments Yearbook*, selected issues.

Table A-3. *Marginal Import Shares*[a] *for Forty-seven Developing Countries from*

Importer	United States	United Kingdom	Aus- tria	Bel- gium	Den- mark	France	Ger- many	Italy	Nether- lands	Nor- way
Latin America										
Argentina	0.237	0.048	0.013	0.011	0.003	0.031	0.013	0.064	0.018	0.003
Bolivia	0.501	0.014	0.041	0.017	0.004	0.031	0.288	0.060	0.064	0.006
Brazil	0.137	0.044	0.000	0.007	0.005	0.026	0.080	0.002	0.009	0.002
Chile	0.141	0.037	0.003	0.017	0.006	0.047	0.067	0.032	0.004	0.025
Colombia	0.041	0.033	0.007	0.012	0.006	0.047	0.104	0.039	0.016	0.000
Costa Rica	0.265	0.037	0.001	0.018	0.003	0.009	0.081	0.016	0.018	0.002
Dominican Republic	0.447	0.041	0.005	0.008	0.009	0.033	0.021	0.063	0.002	0.010
Ecuador	0.449	0.054	0.004	0.006	0.003	0.007	0.042	0.024	0.002	0.003
El Salvador	0.014	0.155	0.011	0.014	0.010	0.007	0.195	0.153	0.003	0.008
Guatemala	0.057	0.052	0.002	0.032	0.012	0.024	0.099	0.003	0.028	0.003
Jamaica	0.454	0.180	0.015	0.000	0.002	0.013	0.035	0.027	0.011	0.000
Mexico	0.619	0.000	0.000	0.008	0.004	0.033	0.084	0.011	0.036	0.007
Panama	0.213	0.033	0.003	0.007	0.015	0.010	0.015	0.010	0.017	0.002
Peru	0.394	0.050	0.004	0.013	0.006	0.019	0.376	0.046	0.023	0.004
Trinidad and Tobago	0.048	0.033	0.000	0.001	0.001	0.002	0.007	0.000	0.001	0.001
Uruguay	0.093	0.098	0.008	0.016	0.006	0.008	0.101	0.029	0.010	0.007
Venezuela	0.073	0.014	0.002	0.013	0.013	0.037	0.056	0.023	0.009	0.005
Middle East										
Egypt	0.060	0.035	0.004	0.004	0.016	0.112	0.093	0.055	0.003	0.007
Iran	0.085	0.083	0.004	0.034	0.006	0.029	0.160	0.032	0.005	0.000
Iraq	0.034	0.066	0.015	0.019	0.000	0.085	0.030	0.011	0.007	0.000
Israel	0.072	0.019	0.000	0.010	0.000	0.017	0.041	0.005	0.003	0.007
Syria	0.092	0.000	0.010	0.028	0.009	0.029	0.059	0.015	0.043	0.000
Asia										
Afghanistan	0.163	0.007	0.004	0.003	0.004	0.022	0.099	0.026	0.028	0.006
Burma	0.025	0.020	0.006	0.005	0.007	0.006	0.088	0.022	0.383	0.042
Cambodia (Khmer Republic)	0.122	0.053	0.002	0.027	0.004	0.369	0.050	0.105	0.043	0.012
India	0.643	0.119	0.005	0.023	0.002	0.065	0.123	0.002	0.018	0.004
Indonesia	0.183	0.056	0.000	0.007	0.000	0.015	0.085	0.006	0.010	0.000
Korea	0.500	0.037	0.001	0.011	0.001	0.043	0.028	0.008	0.009	0.001
Malaysia	0.145	0.064	0.001	0.000	0.000	0.008	0.035	0.002	0.000	0.000
Pakistan	0.455	0.032	0.002	0.028	0.000	0.042	0.144	0.046	0.017	0.009
Philippines	0.308	0.167	0.000	0.000	0.003	0.035	0.254	0.009	0.015	0.009
Sri Lanka	0.171	0.319	0.001	0.000	0.004	0.000	0.050	0.000	0.003	0.002
Thailand	0.074	0.098	0.003	0.025	0.007	0.018	0.645	0.002	0.011	0.002
Vietnam, Republic of	0.375	0.004	0.000	0.003	0.000	0.054	0.007	0.004	0.134	0.000
Africa										
Algeria	0.052	0.075	0.029	0.041	0.004	0.197	0.148	0.108	0.029	0.003
Ghana	0.057	0.141	0.010	0.027	0.018	0.072	0.154	0.036	0.003	0.035
Ivory Coast	0.096	0.019	0.000	0.021	0.009	0.296	0.084	0.137	0.048	0.014
Kenya	0.105	0.271	0.006	0.010	0.008	0.039	0.083	0.036	0.245	0.007
Morocco	0.208	0.047	0.000	0.040	0.004	0.245	0.074	0.095	0.020	0.010
Nigeria	0.177	0.306	0.006	0.029	0.011	0.027	0.155	0.031	0.028	0.000
Senegal	0.111	0.079	0.002	0.003	0.005	0.028	0.032	0.010	0.013	0.003
Sudan	0.000	0.009	0.013	0.005	0.009	0.031	0.086	0.000	0.016	0.002
Tanzania, United Republic of	0.032	0.089	0.002	0.021	0.012	0.008	0.091	0.011	0.041	0.004
Tunisia	0.014	0.032	0.076	0.044	0.077	0.419	0.048	0.064	0.031	0.001
Uganda	0.024	0.078	0.004	0.000	0.002	0.011	0.009	0.017	0.008	0.001
Zaire	0.089	0.080	0.006	0.143	0.009	0.118	0.097	0.040	0.041	0.001
Zambia	0.080	0.266	0.040	0.062	0.009	0.051	0.090	0.028	0.012	0.085

Sources: Calculated from United Nations, *Yearbook of International Trade Statistics*, and International Monetary Fund, *Direction of Trade*, annual issues.

a. The marginal import shares are unadjusted. They are the coefficients from linear regressions of imports from each individual supplier on each purchaser's total imports for the period covered. Negative estimates are suppressed to zero. Text calculations are normalized, requiring the sum of unity across suppliers for a given importer.

Developed Countries, 1967–71

Swe-den	Canada	Japan	Fin-land	Greece	Ireland	Spain	Turkey	Yugo-slavia	Aus-tralia	New Zealand	South Africa
0.015	0.031	0.124	0.000	0.000	0.000	0.012	0.000	0.002	0.025	0.000	0.004
0.055	0.038	0.383	0.020	0.000	0.020	0.020	0.000	0.001	0.000	0.000	0.010
0.010	0.021	0.053	0.001	0.000	0.000	0.007	0.000	0.001	0.000	0.000	0.001
0.007	0.008	0.066	0.003	0.000	0.001	0.019	0.000	0.000	0.011	0.000	0.000
0.020	0.024	0.108	0.002	0.000	0.000	0.003	0.000	0.013	0.000	0.000	0.000
0.016	0.020	0.142	0.003	0.000	0.000	0.021	0.000	0.000	0.000	0.000	0.002
0.008	0.093	0.281	0.001	0.000	0.000	0.036	0.000	0.000	0.000	0.000	0.000
0.002	0.008	0.189	0.005	0.000	0.000	0.230	0.000	0.020	0.006	0.000	0.001
0.032	0.000	0.292	0.004	0.001	0.000	0.002	0.000	0.000	0.000	0.000	0.000
0.005	0.007	0.181	0.004	0.000	0.002	0.012	0.000	0.000	0.000	0.000	0.000
0.012	0.030	0.019	0.001	0.000	0.000	0.000	0.000	0.001	0.011	0.025	0.000
0.003	0.023	0.017	0.006	0.000	0.001	0.019	0.000	0.000	0.013	0.003	0.003
0.007	0.018	0.115	0.000	0.000	0.000	0.006	0.000	0.000	0.007	0.005	0.004
0.016	0.056	0.120	0.005	0.000	0.000	0.002	0.000	0.001	0.011	0.021	0.000
0.000	0.001	0.018	0.001	0.000	0.000	0.000	0.000	0.000	0.000	0.004	0.698
0.040	0.012	0.034	0.003	0.024	0.002	0.058	0.000	0.002	0.003	0.000	0.000
0.003	0.033	0.105	0.004	0.000	0.000	0.029	0.000	0.001	0.003	0.000	0.000
0.019	0.095	0.018	0.000	0.013	0.000	0.043	0.006	0.012	0.244	0.000	0.000
0.010	0.011	0.209	0.012	0.001	0.000	0.019	0.006	0.002	0.046	0.001	0.009
0.028	0.159	0.046	0.004	0.000	0.002	0.016	0.022	0.005	0.114	0.000	0.003
0.002	0.003	0.011	0.003	0.027	0.004	0.002	0.001	0.001	0.000	0.000	0.000
0.029	0.158	0.074	0.000	0.008	0.000	0.014	0.019	0.029	0.000	0.000	0.003
0.002	0.018	0.004	0.000	0.000	0.000	0.000	0.000	0.000	0.001	0.000	0.000
0.004	0.019	0.782	0.019	0.008	0.000	0.003	0.138	0.110	0.066	0.018	0.035
0.058	0.015	0.029	0.001	0.000	0.002	0.018	0.000	0.002	0.000	0.000	0.000
0.017	0.020	0.091	0.000	0.000	0.000	0.007	0.000	0.015	0.074	0.000	0.000
0.000	0.000	0.526	0.000	0.000	0.000	0.000	0.000	0.000	0.033	0.000	0.000
0.000	0.022	0.388	0.000	0.000	0.000	0.000	0.000	0.000	0.019	0.000	0.002
0.004	0.008	0.178	0.000	0.000	0.000	0.000	0.000	0.000	0.038	0.000	0.000
0.003	0.054	0.130	0.000	0.002	0.000	0.002	0.000	0.003	0.041	0.005	0.000
0.012	0.132	0.272	0.002	0.006	0.001	0.001	0.000	0.000	0.061	0.039	0.000
0.016	0.016	0.089	0.000	0.000	0.000	0.001	0.003	0.062	0.000	0.000	0.006
0.007	0.014	0.427	0.003	0.000	0.000	0.003	0.000	0.000	0.055	0.019	0.009
0.003	0.005	0.516	0.002	0.000	0.000	0.000	0.000	0.000	0.019	0.000	0.000
0.013	0.025	0.040	0.007	0.007	0.000	0.048	0.002	0.007	0.000	0.000	0.000
0.001	0.004	0.123	0.005	0.002	0.002	0.019	0.000	0.003	0.000	0.000	0.000
0.009	0.004	0.075	0.003	0.000	0.000	0.016	0.000	0.001	0.000	0.000	0.000
0.015	0.003	0.172	0.001	0.001	0.000	0.004	0.000	0.015	0.030	0.002	0.003
0.044	0.018	0.033	0.004	0.000	0.003	0.091	0.002	0.003	0.000	0.000	0.003
0.010	0.010	0.075	0.000	0.000	0.004	0.000	0.000	0.003	0.004	0.000	0.000
0.005	0.005	0.198	0.000	0.000	0.000	0.001	0.000	0.001	0.046	0.006	0.000
0.017	0.016	0.000	0.001	0.000	0.000	0.005	0.000	0.040	0.108	0.000	0.000
0.034	0.000	0.053	0.002	0.002	0.000	0.005	0.000	0.010	0.006	0.000	0.000
0.030	0.059	0.003	0.000	0.002	0.001	0.040	0.032	0.000	0.000	0.000	0.000
0.003	0.000	0.069	0.000	0.000	0.000	0.000	0.000	0.001	0.004	0.001	0.000
0.001	0.004	0.131	0.001	0.004	0.001	0.011	0.001	0.002	0.000	0.000	0.000
0.290	0.017	0.015	0.010	0.002	0.009	0.017	0.000	0.042	0.052	0.007	0.499

APPENDIX B

A Mathematical Model of Two Effects of the SDR Aid Link

A mathematical model may be used to test the following two hypotheses concerning economic effects of a link between emissions of Special Drawing Rights and development assistance: (1) that a link would aggravate the imbalance of reserves between industrial countries with deficit and surplus balances; and (2) that additional SDR receipts from a link would exacerbate inflation. Chapter 3 reports the results of the simulations conducted with the model. This appendix states the equations, data sources, and assumptions used in the model.

For a given amount of a global SDR emission E, the change in reserves of industrial country i will be:

$$(1) \qquad \Delta R_i = \phi_i E + \sum_j \alpha_{ij} \phi_j E (1 - \gamma_j)$$

where ΔR_i is the change in country i's reserves; α_{ij} is the marginal share of advanced country i in developing country j's imports; and γ_j is the propensity of country j to use incremental foreign receipts for the accumulation of reserves. Also ϕ_k is developing or industrial country k's share in the SDR emission.

The first component on the right-hand side of equation 1 represents direct receipts of SDRs for the industrial country i. The second component represents its indirect receipts derived from increased exports to the LDCs. This magnitude is the sum over all LDCs of the country's share in their marginal imports (α_{ij}) times the increment in importing capacity each received ($\phi_j E$), appropriately reduced to account for leakage of new SDRs into LDC reserves by the factor $(1 - \gamma_j)$.

118

The formulation of equation 1 assumes that developing countries spend most of what they receive in incremental foreign exchange availability whereas advanced countries do not. Hence, indirect SDR earnings in the second term on the right-hand side include only those from LDCs.[1] The concept that LDC imports are directly determined by their exchange availability is well established in the development literature.[2] In contrast, the import functions of advanced countries will depend on variables such as income, prices, and exchange rates, so that the direct effect of SDR receipts will be to increase their reserves (captured in the first term on the right-hand side) rather than their imports.[3]

The propensity of the developing country to accumulate reserves out of foreign exchange receipts, γ_j, may be estimated by considering the following relationships. A realistic rule of thumb is that country j will maintain a given ratio of reserves to imports, β_j.[4] If its trade magnitudes are growing at the rate ρ, then so will its reserves. Thus:

$$\Delta R_j = \rho R_j$$

where ΔR_j is the change in country j's reserves. Since foreign receipts, F, must be exhausted by imports, M, plus reserve accumulation,

$$\Delta R_j + M_j = F_j.$$

If a constant ratio of reserves to imports is maintained at the magnitude β_j, then the propensity to accumulate reserves out of foreign receipts will be:

$$\gamma_j = \frac{\rho R_j}{\rho R_j + (R_j/\beta_j)} = \frac{\rho \beta_j}{1 + \rho \beta_j}.$$

1. The analysis excludes indirect effects concerning LDC imports from other LDCs, which then in turn import from industrial countries. This intramural trading is limited, and the empirical analysis below adjusts the estimated parameters so that there is no SDR "leakage" due to exclusion of trading among LDCs.

2. Hollis B. Chenery and Alan M. Strout, "Foreign Assistance and Economic Development," *American Economic Review*, vol. 56 (1966), pp. 679–733; and William L. Hemphill, "The Effect of Foreign Exchange Receipts on Imports of Less Developed Countries" (Princeton University; processed, 1974).

3. If there were a large divergence between the pattern of SDR allocation and demand for reserves, it is likely that an indirect effect of the emissions would be to change the advanced country's exchange rate, thereby affecting its imports and exports. Under a balanced distribution, however, no such changes would occur, since no one currency would be strengthened relative to others.

4. As noted by Williamson, the notion of a constant ratio of reserves to imports is well established in the literature on international liquidity, although the literature

In the analysis below, β_j is calculated from actual data on average reserves and imports over a five-year period; a standard trade growth rate of $\rho = 0.06$ is then applied to estimate the expected propensity to accumulate reserves.[5]

Given equation 1, it is possible to examine the impact of an SDR aid link by varying the distributional pattern for SDRs, raising the shares ϕ_k for developing countries and lowering them for advanced countries. Similarly, the impact of alternative SDR distributional schemes may be examined for advanced country exports, LDC imports, and LDC reserves. Thus:

$$(2) \qquad \Delta X_i = \sum_j \alpha_{ij}\phi_j E(1 - \gamma_j)$$

---

includes much more complicated approaches to optimal reserve behavior. John Williamson, "Surveys in Applied Economics: International Liquidity," *Economic Journal*, vol. 83 (September 1973), pp. 685–746.

5. The estimation of reserve accumulation propensity abstracts from the 30 percent reconstitution requirement for SDRs (which provides that over a five-year period the average balance held must be no less than 30 percent of the SDR allocation received). In fact, the estimated values of γ_j are in the neighborhood of 2 percent with the maximum observed value being 4 percent. This apparent discrepancy is not bothersome. Reserves of various types are fungible, and SDRs will generally constitute a sufficiently small portion of total reserves that it will be possible for the country to retain 30 percent of SDR receipts without altering the desired ratio of reserves to imports by spending rather than holding a sufficiently larger portion of other foreign exchange receipts. Of course, if a link were adopted it would be appropriate to eliminate the 30 percent reconstitution provision for SDRs linked to aid because the objective would be to transfer resources through the spending of these SDRs.

LDC reserves have grown quite rapidly in recent years. Between 1970 and 1972 reserves of LDCs rose by the same proportion (60 percent) as total world reserves. From the beginning of 1972 through August of 1974, however, LDC reserves practically doubled whereas the world total rose by only 18 percent (International Monetary Fund, *International Financial Statistics* [IMF, selected issues]). Excluding oil exporters (whose reserves tripled) LDC reserves still grew by 39 percent during the period. The rapid 1970–72 accumulation reflects general expansion of world reserves associated with dollar outflows. The 1972–74 accumulation reflects extraordinary commodity price increases in 1973 and 1974, and these windfall reserves will no doubt be drawn upon heavily to pay higher oil import bills. Over the longer run the assumption in the analysis—that LDCs will accumulate only enough reserves to maintain constant their reserve-import ratios—should be much more appropriate than any propensity to accumulate reserves that might be calculated on the basis of recent experience.

where ΔX_i is the increase of advanced country i's exports attributable to SDR emissions in the amount E;

(3) $$\Delta R_j = \gamma_j \phi_j\, E$$

where ΔR_j is the change in developing country j's reserves after an SDR emission; and

(4) $$\Delta M_j = \phi_j E(1 - \gamma_j)$$

where ΔM_j is the change in developing country j's imports after the emission.

Once again the impact of shifting the basis for SDR allocation from the quota system of the International Monetary Fund to an aid link may be explored through applying varying SDR share profiles, ϕ_j, to equations 2, 3, and 4.

To estimate the model empirically, data for forty-seven less developed and twenty-two developed countries have been used. The LDCs examined include all those having IMF quotas of 30 million SDRs or greater,[6] and account for 91 percent of total SDRs allocated to developing countries in the first allocation period, 1970–72. The developed countries considered account for 99.7 percent of SDRs allocated to advanced countries.

Trade data for the 1967–71 period[7] are used to estimate the marginal trade propensities, α_{ij}, for each LDC. These parameters are estimated by linear regressions of the form:

$$M_{ijt} = a_{ij} + \alpha_{ij}M_{jt} + u_{ijt}$$

where M_{ijt} denotes imports into developing country j from advanced country i in year t in value terms; M_{jt} denotes total imports of LDC j, year t in value terms, and u_{ijt} is the error term.

To adjust for the fact that some countries, both developing and developed, are left out of the analysis, the estimated value $\hat{\alpha}_{ij}$ is normalized to:

$$\alpha_{ij} = \hat{\alpha}_{ij}/(\sum_i \hat{\alpha}_{ij}),$$

6. The corresponding magnitude of SDR allocations over the 1970–72 period was a cutoff amount of 3 million SDRs. Certain countries, both developing and advanced, are excluded from the analysis because they did not participate in the Special Drawing Rights scheme. All of the analysis is conducted using IMF quotas prevailing before the 1975 quota revision agreement which increased the share of oil-exporting countries at the expense of that of the industrial countries.

7. From the following sources: United Nations, *Yearbook of International Trade Statistics,* and International Monetary Fund, *Direction of Trade,* annual issues.

so that the sum of marginal import shares is forced to unity. In this way, leakage to countries not considered in the model does not give a downward bias to the estimates of indirect reserve earnings of developed countries. Moreover, the adjustment takes account of the fact that the individual marginal trade share regression coefficients may sum to more than unity.[8]

As an alternative procedure, it is assumed that the marginal import shares equal average shares:

$$\bar{\alpha}_{ij} = \bar{M}_{ij}/\sum_i \bar{M}_{ij}$$

where $\bar{M}_{ij}$ is the five-year average of imports into developing country j from developed country i.

This alternative serves as a check on the reliability of the regression estimates. The average share is also normalized to refer only to the set of countries examined; only imports from these twenty-two developed countries are considered in country j's total imports.

For calculation of the reserve-import ratios, β_j, total beginning-of-the-year reserves[9] for the five-year period 1967–71 are divided by total imports of goods and services during the same period.[10]

The initial SDR distribution shares ϕ_k are calculated directly from data on SDR allocations received by each country during 1970–72.[11]

The preceding equations constitute the full model of the effects of linking SDR emissions to aid on payments imbalances and inflation. The findings from the calculations using the model are discussed in chapter 3.

8. Furthermore, regression coefficients α_{ij} that are negative are suppressed to zero, since a negative marginal trade share is unacceptable.

9. Reported in International Monetary Fund, *International Financial Statistics.*

10. Reported in International Monetary Fund, *Balance of Payments Yearbook.*

11. As reported in *International Financial Statistics.* Note that for developed countries, a very minor upward adjustment is made to absorb the share of Malta (excluded from direct analysis). For the LDCs, the SDR share is adjusted upward proportionately to absorb the shares of those participating LDCs not treated directly in the analysis.

Index

Alliance for Progress, 6
Articles of Agreement, IMF, amendments to, 5, 9n, 89, 91n, 99n
Asian Development Bank, Special Fund, 78

Balance of payments: currency reserves accumulation and, 2; effect of currency devaluation on, 10; effect of oil prices on, 5; flexible exchange rates for adjusting, 4, 8, 96, 109; under gold standard, 1; SDR aid link and, 67–68, 72, 75, 76
Barber, Anthony, 13n
Bergsten, C. Fred, 3n, 65n
Blackhurst, Richard, 19n
Black, Stanley W., 25n
Bretton Woods system, 2–3, 7, 18, 49, 50, 70–71
Business cycles, SDR aid link and, 71–72

Campos, A. Roberto, 28n, 32n
Capital flow, 8, 45; controls over, 20; exchange rate flexibility and, 34–35
Cline, William R., 94n
Cohen, Benjamin J., 73
Columbo, Emilio, 56, 61n
Committee on Reform of the International Monetary System. See Committee of Twenty
Committee of Twenty, 3, 75n; delegates to, 3n–4n; issues considered by, 4; LDC participation in, 6, 12, 49, 110; SDR aid link and, 49, 50, 63, 73, 78, 110
Connolly, Michael B., 10
Convertibility of currencies: under gold

exchange standard, 1, 2; under gold standard, 1; into reserve assets, 4
Cooper, Richard N., 10
Crawling peg, 11
Currencies: blocs, 40–41; convertibility of, 1, 2, 4; pegging of, 23–25, 40–44, 46

Dell, Sidney, 70n, 72, 74n
Development assistance: international liquidity and, 50–57; "untied," 60. See also SDR aid link
Díaz-Alejandro, Carlos F., 26n
Dollar: LDC currency pegged to, 40, 41, 43, 44, 46; devaluation of, 5, 8, 18, 37, 38–40, 47; LDC reserves and, 38, 47; LDC trade balance and, 38–40
Domestic International Sales Corporation, 69n

Eurodollar market, 29, 101, 104n
Exchange rates: balance of payments and, 2, 4; during depression of 1930s, 1–2; devaluation of, 10; inflation and, 10, 20; risk aversion analysis of, 15–20. See also Fixed exchange rates; Flexible exchange rates; Floating exchange rates; Smithsonian agreement for realignment of exchange rates
Exports: LDC, 10, 35–37, 73

Fixed exchange rates, 2, 9; compared with flexible rates, 29; permanent versus periodic realignments of, 14–15
Fleming, J. Marcus, 20
Flexible exchange rates, 2; balance of payments and, 4, 8, 71, 96, 109; Com-